LONE A MEMOIR HOLDOUT

LINDA COX

CHARLES STREET PRESS

BOSTON

Library of Congress Control Number: 2010901185

ISBN: 978-0-9843733-0-7

Charles Street Press, P.O. Box 328, Charles Street Station, Boston, MA 02114

www.charlesstreetpress.com

Book and cover design: Joanne Legge

Text set in Plantin and Helvetica Neue

To my mother, Helen Sipes Cox

AUTHOR'S NOTE

Lone Holdout is a true story. It is based on my notes and memory and those of others, as well as newspaper stories and court transcripts. Material in quotation marks in courtroom scenes is taken directly from official transcripts of the proceedings. The names of the jurors have been changed, as have the name and physical description of David the banker. Any other names that have been changed are noted with quotation marks the first time they are used. I have not knowingly taken any other liberties with the truth, but like all true stories, *Lone Holdout* has ambiguities and loose ends.

prologue

I STARED INTO THE ACCUSED man's dark eyes one more time. Carlos Montilla, charged with cocaine trafficking and carrying an illegal firearm, sat at the defendant's table between his pudgy, middle-aged lawyer and the dark-haired young woman who was translating into his ear. He met my eyes for several seconds, as he often had before, and then looked away. I was one of the jurors who would determine his fate.

Police Officer Albert LaFontaine, the sole material witness against Montilla, sat at the prosecutor's table next to the young female district attorney. He turned his head toward the jury box and smiled.

After three days of testimony in the stifling oak-paneled courtroom, the gray-haired judge was reading us our instructions. Our verdict must be unanimous.

"The jury may retire to deliberate," announced the clerk. It was ten minutes to eleven on a Friday morning in July. The twelve of us trooped up a back staircase from the courtroom to the floor above and walked into jury room 860.

At four o'clock that afternoon, after five hours of bitter wrangling, we were sent home by the judge and told to return on Monday with open minds. All of the jurors but one had agreed on a verdict. I was the one.

one

WHEN I REPORTED FOR JURY duty in the middle of the hottest summer on record in Boston, I was securely planted in my sheltered world. I had lived and worked for more than twenty years on Beacon Hill, an historic neighborhood of early 1800s brick townhouses, tree-lined streets, brick sidewalks, gaslights, and a skyline of slate roofs and chimney pots. At the bottom of the Hill, the Charles River glints into view; in the other direction, the State House dome gleams gold. Beacon Hill was no longer an enclave of Boston Brahmins, and many residents, like me, were far from rich; yet the neighborhood still had an air of privilege.

It was my adopted home. The oldest of five children, I was born and raised in Tulsa, Oklahoma, except for a few years in West Texas where my father worked as an oil engineer. After my father's death, by his own hand, when I was thirteen, my mother moved us back to Tulsa. She received several offers to adopt us; my sister and I would have gone to one family, our three brothers to another. Mother would not hear of it. This former college beauty queen and honor-society member could type and take shorthand, and she raised the five of us on a secretary's salary. Money was always tight, but somehow we never felt poor.

When I won a scholarship to Wellesley College, "back East," Mother was determined that I would go there. It was not a full scholarship that first year, and we did not have the money for the rest of the tuition and board. One night she woke me out of a deep sleep to say, "I have decided that no matter what you are going to Wellesley." Before she could rob a bank or whatever she had in mind, her rich relatives came through, unasked, with the necessary funds. These relatives were among those who had offered to adopt my sister and me; this offer she could accept.

I fell in love with New England and chose to live in Boston after I graduated. My sister and brothers all stayed in Tulsa; I was the only one who flew the nest. Mother missed having me close by, but she enjoyed coming to visit and traveling abroad with me. After a few years in Cambridge working as a secretary, I took an editorial position with a Boston publisher and moved to Beacon Hill. I stayed in publishing for twelve years, until I changed careers. I didn't think I had a future at the publishing company — I was one of the five named plaintiffs in a successful class-action sex discrimination case — and I had received an irresistible proposition.

One cold January morning, a month after the class-action suit had been settled in our favor, my friend Sue Timken called me. I had met Sue when we both worked at the publishing company, and we remained friends after she became bored and left the job; independently wealthy, she did not have to work.

"How would you like to have a bookstore with me?" Sue asked. "I think we'd be perfect partners. I'm rich, and you're conscientious."

Sue was not just rich, of course. She had a keen mind (Phi Beta Kappa, Smith College), a compassionate heart, and a wicked sense of humor. Her quick, dry wit was fueled by her love of words and a strong irreverent streak. Shy and self-effacing, she had a formidable will when she set her mind to something — like having a bookstore with me to give structure to her life.

Sue and I both loved words and books. One of my earliest memories is the acute longing to be able to read. I had memorized all the books that were read aloud to me, and I would hold them and recite the words, pretending to read. Most of the adults in my life were convinced that I really could read, although my mother was not fooled. On my first day in first grade, I looked around at the combinations of letters that were posted on the upper walls of the room, and I had the strongest sense of exhilaration in my life. "Here is the key that will unlock the words," I silently exulted, my blood racing.

From then on, I almost always had my nose in a book. I was lost in another world, unaware of the passing of time, deaf to anyone who spoke to me. I read anything I could get my hands on, from cover to cover. I would sound out unfamiliar words, saying them over and over until they tasted right. When I was in the third grade, my mother allowed me to go by myself to the nearby public library, my card, like a passport, clutched in my hand. I vowed to read every book in the children's section, alphabetically by author. I know I got through all of Louisa May Alcott's books, but I can't remember any further than that — fadeout after *Jo's Boys*. Later I became less voracious and more selective, and currently I was savoring the novels of Austen, Eliot, and Trollope, occasionally leavened by P.G. Wodehouse or Dorothy Sayers. Books were an integral, cherished part of my life. Of course I jumped at Sue's offer.

Neither of us book-lovers knew anything about bookselling, but fools rush in. Less than two months later, after looking at several rental locations, we heard by chance that our twenty-five-year-old neighborhood bookshop was for sale. Located in a townhouse on a residential street, the store was a beloved Beacon Hill institution. Someone else was on the verge of buying it, but we offered more. Within a week of learning the store was for sale, we were the new owners.

Our ground-floor shop, entered through an alley, was a cozy, carpeted space, with two rooms and an alcove. The brick walls, some painted white, were covered with shelves from the low ceiling to the floor. Books were everywhere — on shelves, on tables, even stacked on the floor. In the front room, where we had quality fiction and nonfiction, there was a street-level picture window to display books, a desk for the bookseller on duty, and a counter for the cash register. An alcove, with a window onto a small patio, held a second desk, where I often sat to do paperwork. The back room, devoted mostly to paperbacks and children's books, was a popular spot for young customers and their mothers. Classical music played all day on the radio.

Through the bookstore and my volunteer work in the neighborhood association, I knew many people on the Hill. I moved in a friendly, approving, almost small-town orbit, greeted by name on the street and in the small shops I frequented. In the morning I walked across the street to a European-style café where the young Irish girl knew what I wanted and brought it to me without my asking: cappuccino in a large cup, heaped with extra foam like a soufflé. At ten the bookstore opened, and I did my work there while enjoying the company of a witty business partner and mostly congenial customers, many of whom had become friends.

Single, I lived alone in a one-bedroom apartment above the bookstore. Between my work and my circle of friends I was never lonely. I enjoyed my solitary moments, especially the long walks I took almost every day along the Charles River Esplanade. In warmer months my goal was a stand of wild roses near the Boston University Bridge; having reached it, I bent to smell one of the dark-pink blossoms. The flowers had almost no fragrance, but the ritual pleased me. If there were thorns, I did not notice.

But perhaps my life had been too pleasant for too long. Under the serene surface, I was growing restless. It was as if I were marking time, waiting for something to happen. I didn't know what I was waiting for or what I wanted, and I never would have guessed the dramatic turn my life was about to take.

The jury summons, my first ever, came in April 1988 for an inconvenient date in June. I postponed it until a Tuesday in the middle of July, hoping that nothing would be happening in court — I didn't want the bother of serving on a jury. And if that didn't work I was sure I'd be challenged anyway; the class-action lawsuit was duly noted on my juror's questionnaire. "They won't touch me with a ten-foot pole," I told Sue. We chuckled over the earnest text of my juror's handbook, a tan pamphlet with an amateurish cover drawing of blindfolded Justice holding her scales.

It was an easy ten-minute walk from my apartment to the Suffolk County Courthouse, a granite Greek Revival pile adorned with colonnades, pediments, balconies, and a clock.

I was ordered to appear in the "new" courthouse added on in 1937, an Art Deco monolith of gray stone and brick. As I walked into the entrance at 8:30 that Tuesday morning, I didn't notice the bas relief and inscription over the door: Justice for All. A photographer pointed it out to me almost two years later.

We prospective jurors were brought into courtroom 815 and sat down on the wooden benches in the back of the high-ceilinged, oak-paneled room. Behind the judge's bench, an inset bookcase was filled with law books; over it hung a portrait of a gray-haired, middle-aged judge in black robes who looked remarkably like the man actually sitting on the bench, Judge Walter Steele, except our judge was wearing glasses.

When I was finally called to the box, I perched on the edge of the swivel chair, ready to leave quickly when I was excused. The defense attorney glanced up at me as he read my question-naire, and I met his bright blue eyes. I don't think the prose-cutor even looked at me. Then the clerk announced, "We have a jury," and I sat there stunned. I was juror number nine in a drug-dealing trial.

The case had seemed so simple in the beginning, when the charges were read to us before jury selection. A young Hispanic man was accused of drug trafficking and carrying an illegal fire-arm, and three police officers were testifying against him — it sounded straight out of "Miami Vice." But as I listened to the opening statements after the lunch break, I began to question my assumption that the defendant was probably guilty; it did not sound to me like an open-and-shut case. I was all attention, determined to search for the truth as hard as I could. I wanted to be a good juror.

Officer Albert LaFontaine was the first prosecution witness. He swore to tell the truth and strutted to the stand. A slight, middle-aged man, he was dressed in a loose sports shirt, khaki pants, and scuffed cowboy boots. He had receding dark-brown hair, small brown eyes, and a pale moustache that blended into his face. Deep creases furrowed his high forehead and framed his nose and mouth like parentheses. A Boston police officer for sixteen years, LaFontaine did undercover narcotics work.

Almost as soon as LaFontaine began to speak, I had an uncomfortable feeling about him. It was nothing I could put my finger on, but I was on high alert as I listened to his testimony.

Assistant District Attorney Lynn Beland, a thirtyish woman with short streaked hair and broad, hunched shoulders, stood at the microphone at the end of the jury box railing and took LaFontaine through the story outlined in her opening statement: Two years previously, on the night of October 1, LaFontaine and his partner, Edward Fleming, had stationed themselves in a school parking lot across the street and about a hundred yards away from the Geneva Avenue housing project, where they had received a tip that drug deals were going on. They began their observations, LaFontaine said, about 7:30 or 8:00, and the lighting conditions were very good. Through binoculars, he observed two people outside #223 apparently dealing drugs. One of the men was Pablo Osario, who was known to them; the other was "the gentleman right there in front of us."

"And would you point to the person?" Beland asked.

LaFontaine pointed to Carlos Montilla, the young man who sat at the defendant's table between his attorney and the interpreter. His eyes were fixed on LaFontaine, but his head was tilted toward the woman who was translating for him.

He was good-looking, with black hair and luminous dark eyes. A tidy moustache emphasized his full, almost pouty, lower lip. He looked confused, expectant, and very young.

LaFontaine looked straight into Montilla's eyes and smiled. "He had, like a Michael Jackson hairstyle, jeans. That's about it."

Under more questioning, LaFontaine testified that he saw people come up to Montilla, converse, give him money, and wait while Montilla went upstairs and returned with a packet. Between transactions, he said, Montilla and Osario "would turn around and joke, laugh, like they knew each other for a long time." After observing about seven cars pull in, LaFontaine moved across the street and hid behind the bushes near the dumpsters in the project's parking lot. From there, still using binoculars, he observed at least two more transactions.

"Now during that time did you have the defendant in your view?"

"Yes, ma'am."

"And did you see him from all angles?"

"Yes, ma'am." LaFontaine said these "Yes, ma'ams" with elaborate courtesy.

His testimony continued: he and Fleming left about 8:30 to answer a radio call, returning to the project sometime later. Osario and Montilla were no longer in sight. When LaFontaine spotted three black males entering the apartment building at #223, he told Fleming to cover the rear while he went in the front. He entered the building, went up the stairs, and tried to listen.

Beland asked him to describe the stairway as it was on the night of the incident. (Before lunch, we jurors had visited the scene of the alleged crime, a decaying housing project of three-story brick buildings. Because #223 was now boarded up, we had viewed the stairs in an adjacent, supposedly identical building. We had stepped two or three at a time into the tiny hall to look at the narrow stairway, of which we could see only the first five steps up to a landing.)

The stairs, LaFontaine said, were made of concrete with metal supports. "And you could see right through the stairs."

"What did you observe?"

"I observed three black males that had gone in previous to my entering the hallway." He was on the second-floor level, he said, and could see up through the stairs.

Beland said, "Okay. Now when you turned at that second-floor level, did you see the defendant?"

Yes, he had seen the defendant, inside the apartment; the door was open about eighteen to twenty inches. One of the black males was in the middle of the door talking to the defendant, and two were on each side of the door. Their backs were turned to LaFontaine. The defendant was facing LaFontaine, about ten feet away. He was the same fellow he had seen outside with Osario. He could see the whole body of the defendant. Beland asked LaFontaine to describe Montilla.

"The defendant had black hair, very greasy type, Michael Jackson with the little curls. And he was completely nude except for short underwear, red with black lines." (*It seemed strange to me that someone would go inside, take off his clothes, and continue to deal drugs.*)

"Now did the defendant's hair look like it is today?" I looked again at Montilla — his hair was short, curly, and well groomed. "No ma'am," LaFontaine answered.

"Did you stay there and watch for a while?" Beland asked.

"No, it was a very short time. One of the black males turned and yelled 'Five-O.'"

"And do you know what 'Five-O' means?"

"Police."

"Some things haven't changed," Judge Steele quipped, to general laughter. Beland continued, smiling. "When somebody yelled 'Five-O,' what happened?"

"Everyone runs."

"What happened on this particular —"

"Everybody ran." More laughter. LaFontaine was grinning.

Beland backed up to ask about the conversation LaFontaine had overheard. The three black males, LaFontaine said, were trying to offer Montilla twenty dollars for a forty-dollar bag of drugs. "Montilla was shaking his head, saying no, no, no. And then 'Five-O' rang out. I ran up the stairs, and the black males just ran past me." Then, he said, "I hit the doorway with my shoulder."

"Now was Montilla at that doorway?"

"He was still in front. Yeah." *(Wait a minute, I thought. Montilla was still standing there? Why hadn't he slammed the door when the black males yelled 'Five-O'?)*

"And what happened when you hit the door?"

"When I hit the door I noticed there was a big, heavy, thick chain on the door. I couldn't squeeze my body through. The door was solid. I couldn't go any further."

"And so when the door wouldn't open, what in fact did you do?"

"I pulled my gun out. I had my service revolver in hand. And I pointed it inside the door."

"In fact was your gun out previously? When did you take your gun out?"

"When I started going up the stairs." *(So the three black males had run down those narrow stairs past a policeman with a drawn revolver? It didn't make sense.)*

LaFontaine described putting his head, part of his shoulder, his service revolver, and his hand inside the door and seeing Montilla about four feet in front of him with a gun in his hand. "I pointed my gun at him. His hand went up, pointed at me. I yelled, 'Freeze. Police. I'll shoot.' He dropped the gun, turned around, and headed toward the kitchen area."

LaFontaine radioed his partner that the suspect was going his way and then called for assistance: "If anybody's got a hammer or anything — I have to break a chain." Several officers responded in a few minutes, and two in plain clothes arrived with a hammer. "At that time," LaFontaine testified, "we were able to break the chain and enter."

"Did you see the defendant at the back of the apartment?" Beland asked.

"I went to the back. And I observed the door that led out to the rear was heavily bolted from the inside."

"Did you make any observations at the kitchen where the defendant may have gone?"

"There was a window open. It's approximately maybe four feet by three feet wide. The top portion was open."

LaFontaine then radioed the suspect's description over the air; it was 9:30 or 10:00 p.m., he said. On a table in the front room, he found tinfoil packets, plastic baggies, a strainer and other narcotics paraphernalia, and money. He also picked up the gun, opened it, and saw it was fully loaded. Beland presented to LaFontaine the evidence found in the apartment, and he identified the drugs, the certificates of analysis, an envelope containing $940, and the gun, a Smith and Wesson .38.

As he spoke, LaFontaine toyed with the gun, turning it over and over in his hands until the judge asked, "Could you please point that away from the bench?" Many people laughed, but I did not. These moments of levity seemed inappropriate, as if the judge and prosecutors were buddies.

It was now about three o'clock. Despite the high ceilings, the oak-paneled courtroom was getting hotter by the minute. The two small air conditioners had been turned off during testimony because they were too noisy. A court officer, using a long pole, opened several casements in the tall windows, but that gave little relief. Everyone looked wilted. The clerk, who was wearing a thick black toupee, seemed particularly miserable. I could feel my legs steaming inside my nylons and resolved: tomorrow, bare legs.

Beland continued her questioning, her face flushed a bright pink, her streaked hair damp on her forehead. She asked LaFontaine to describe the papers and identification found in the apartment.

"From Mr. Montilla, we saw, like a pay stub on the floor."

Beland frowned and repeated the question. "Now where was the pay stub?"

"This was on top of the table."

"I now show you a piece of paper and ask if you can recognize it."

LaFontaine took the paper in his hand and looked at it, holding it away from him. "Yes, ma'am. This is the one I recovered from the apartment." It looked like a pay stub of earnings, he said, marked with Montilla's name.

LaFontaine then testified that after about twenty minutes inside the apartment, he and Fleming went back to the station, where they later heard that two officers had a suspect for them to identify. LaFontaine remained at the station making out the inventory report until Fleming and two other officers returned with the suspect, who was fully clothed.

"And when you saw the defendant, what happened?"

"I positively ID'd him."

"What did you say?"

"That's him. That's the guy I saw up there. No doubt."

"How much time had passed from the time you saw the defendant with the gun until you saw him at the station?"

"I'd say probably about half an hour, maybe three-quarters."

"Now what happened when you said, 'That's him'?"

"I placed him under arrest. At that time I'm going to make a search of his body for weapons or property. I then asked him to please remove his pants."

"And what happened?"

"He refused. I informed him if he didn't remove his pants, I would physically do it for him."

"And then what happened?"

LaFontaine crossed his arms and almost laughed as he answered: "Then he complied with my wishes."

Something in the smile that played around LaFontaine's mouth as he spoke these words made me shudder. In that hot room, a chill ran through me.

"And he dropped his pants?" Beland pursued.

"He dropped his pants," LaFontaine responded, with that same chilling smirk. He then identified the underwear he had taken from the defendant. It was the same underwear, he said, that the suspect in the apartment was wearing.

Beland asked another question, but Judge Steele interrupted. "When are you going to finish?" he asked. "It's awfully hot." Beland's eyes widened and she looked a little flustered. "Judge,

I have no problem recessing now and continuing. I have a little bit more."

"All right," the judge agreed. "We will be in recess. It is too hot in here." He told us jurors to be back promptly at ten in the morning and instructed us not to make any firm decisions yet or discuss the case with anyone.

It was close to four o'clock when I returned to the bookstore, where Sue was holding the fort. She sat at the front desk with her head bent over the new Robert Parker mystery, her soft brown hair almost hiding her face. She looked relieved when she saw it was me and not a customer.

"The good news is that I'm not sequestered," I told her. "The bad news is that I'm on a drug trial and I don't know how long it will take."

"And you said they wouldn't touch you with a ten-foot pole," she quipped. I was on the verge of telling her about the case, despite the judge's instructions, when the UPS man came in with a package for a neighbor. By the time he left, the temptation to talk had passed. "I'm sorry to leave you in the lurch," I told Sue. Luckily, it was a slow season for the bookstore, and my absence wouldn't matter that much.

That night I could not stop thinking about LaFontaine's smirk as he said the words "he complied with my wishes." Something in his smile had startled and repelled me. It could have been a trick of the imagination, merely a harmless shadow, not at all what it seemed to be. But I did not trust him.

two

THE NEXT MORNING THE FOURTEEN of us, twelve plus two alternates, gathered in jury room 860, up a back staircase from our courtroom. A large wooden table stood in the middle of the carpeted room, with chairs around it and against the wall. An ancient air conditioner chugged away in one of the two large, multi-paned windows. As in the courtroom, bluish light from fluorescent ceiling fixtures made the room look even dingier than it was.

I chatted with the two men who had shared my *Boston Globe* the day before. Ralph, a tall, light-haired man, volunteered that he was a Republican, and I counter-confessed that I was a liberal. Aaron, who had been appointed foreman after the jury was selected, turned out to be an accountant, and he looked professional, with dark hair and a well-groomed moustache. He and Ralph, the only two of the five men wearing suits, both seemed to be about forty.

Janice, an editor with a small Boston publisher, had been into my bookstore a few times, but it took us a while to figure out where we had seen each other before. She had beautiful greenish-blue eyes behind large glasses that tended to slip down her nose. Cassie, who carried the current *New Yorker* under her arm, was an attractive, well-dressed teacher who lived in Dorchester with her husband and children. She sat next to me in the jury box but kept to herself and said very little.

Curt, around thirty, had dark-blonde hair and wore pale-rimmed glasses. As soon as I heard him speak, I noticed the sarcastic edge to his voice. Another young man, Vincent, fretted that jury duty might interfere with a white-water rafting trip he had planned for the weekend. Joey, young and sullen, and Maureen, a silent blonde girl also in her early twenties, obviously knew each other and were always together. (I later learned that they were brother and sister, highly irregular for a jury.) Esther, very plump and clearly bored by the trial, was the only black person on the jury. Dorothy was a small, dark-haired mother who lived in Dorchester with her family. Although she was only thirty or so, her face had a tight, worried expression.

A grandmotherly woman named Mildred could have been excused because of her age but had chosen not to be. Tricia, tall, lovely, and blond, was in her twenties. Ruth, a fortyish businesswoman who wore skirt suits, also lived in Dorchester with her family. I assumed that she, Cassie, and Dorothy lived in the safer, gentrified sections of this crime-ridden neighborhood.

Shortly after ten o'clock, the court officer lined us up in the hallway, calling off our first names in the order of our seats. We filed down the metal stairs and through a special entrance into the courtroom. The judge greeted us: "Good morning, Mr. Foreman and ladies and gentlemen. It is a little cooler today, but not much."

As LaFontaine resumed the stand, again casually dressed in a loose shirt, I studied him intently. I wanted to be sure my imagination hadn't tricked me the day before.

Beland quickly finished her questioning and sat down. Warren Blair, the defense attorney, rose from the defendant's table and replaced her at the microphone on the jury box railing. He was around forty, with blonde-going-gray hair. "Officer LaFontaine, I'd like to pick up the cross-examination at the time you first observed the three black males going into the building."

"You would like what, sir?" Now wary and almost contemptuous in his manner, LaFontaine had shed the elaborate courtesy of his "Yes, ma'ams" to the prosecutor.

Slowly, like pulling teeth, Blair extracted more or less the same testimony we had heard the day before: Looking up through the stairs from the second floor, LaFontaine saw three black males having a conversation with Montilla about the price of drugs. LaFontaine was spotted — he already had his gun drawn — and charged the door. He radioed his partner that the suspect was coming out the back door.

"And your partner will say that he was there ready for him?" Blair asked.

"That's correct."

"And, in fact, the suspect never came out the back door. We don't know how the suspect got out of the apartment."

"He went out the window, sir," LaFontaine said, contemptuously.

"He went out the window," Blair repeated, as if incredulous.

"That's correct, sir."

"You didn't see him do that. But you just concluded that because there was no other way out; is that it?"

"I kept constant view on that kitchen. He never came out of the kitchen."

"But you never saw him go out the window. You just assumed that."

"Right, sir. There was only that one back door and one window. And the window was open."

Blair asked a few more questions, leading up to the exhibits found in the apartment, and grilled LaFontaine to establish that he had not actually seen in Montilla's hands any of the items entered into evidence. "Now the gun," Blair continued. "You claim you saw the defendant in the apartment with a gun, right?"

"That's correct." The suspect had pointed the gun at him, but he didn't know for how long. "It seemed like a long time, but I couldn't tell you." He was looking at both the gun and the suspect's underwear, he said.

"Did you ever do any fingerprint analysis on anything in the apartment that you took?"

"No, sir."

"You didn't do any fingerprint analysis?"

"I am not a fingerprint expert, sir."

"Okay. You could have something fingerprinted if you wanted to, could you not?"

"For that you have to go in town. And they would not allow me to do that, sir."

"No matter what you wanted to do, you wouldn't be able to do it?" Blair asked, and LaFontaine answered, "No, sir." (*That seemed implausible to me.*)

Blair asked how much time had elapsed from the time that the suspect dropped the gun until he was arrested. "I have no idea, sir," LaFontaine answered. (*But yesterday he had told the prosecutor half an hour or so when she asked him the same question.*)

"You have no idea of that?"

"I have no idea what time —"

"Was it an hour or two?"

"I wasn't looking at the time when he dropped the gun, and I wasn't looking at the time when he was picked up."

"Well, one thing we know —"

"I had other things to do than look at my watch, sir," LaFontaine snapped. "I'm sorry."

Later Blair had LaFontaine retrace his steps during the evening, and again we heard what had become a litany whenever LaFontaine was asked about the time.

LaFontaine: I can't tell you the exact time, no.

Blair: Okay. It was minutes, I take it?

LaFontaine: It could have been.

Blair: Was it hours?

LaFontaine: It could have been. I don't know.

Blair: It could have been hours?

LaFontaine: It could have been.

As I listened to LaFontaine evade Blair's questions, both my instincts and my skeptical mind were in full cry. *Why wouldn't LaFontaine be pinned down, even on questions he had answered straightforwardly when the prosecutor asked them? Why was he being so slippery?* Again, I sensed the ripple under the surface that had so disturbed me the day before. *What was really going on here?*

I turned my attention to the man LaFontaine was accusing, watching him intently for several minutes. Montilla listened to the interpreter with his head bent down almost to his shoulder; he slumped; he fidgeted; he yawned; he looked expectantly at his attorney as Blair tried to extract answers from LaFontaine. Then, as if he felt my eyes on him, Montilla looked toward me, and I stared into the luminous eyes of a bewildered child. He held my gaze for several moments, until I looked back to

LaFontaine on the witness stand. There, clear as day, I saw the face of a liar.

In the moist heat of the courtroom, Blair's curly hair was springing up in little ringlets. His electric blue eyes looked even brighter in his flushed face. The sleeves of his seersucker suit rode up on his arms, revealing bare, plump wrists, as he showed LaFontaine the pay stub allegedly found in the apartment. "I believe you testified yesterday that was on the table, is that correct?"

"That's where I found it."

"That's where you found it. Did anybody have it before you, any other police officer?"

"Could have been, sir." (*Was LaFontaine being careless or simply obstructive?*)

"In any event, you found it on the table, right?"

"Yes, sir."

"Did you do any fingerprints on that particular exhibit?"

"On paper, sir?"

"Yes, on paper. Did you do any fingerprints on it?"

"Only the FBI can remove fingerprints. We are not equipped with that kind of equipment, sir." (*Only the FBI can remove fingerprints? That wasn't true, was it?*)

"There was nothing else in the entire apartment that had his name on it, just that stub, right?"

"That's correct, sir."

"When you placed him under arrest, what did he have on his person?"

"He had a lot of gold chains, fifty dollars. That's it."

"Did he have a wallet?"

"No wallet. No identification. No nothing, sir."

"Now you previously testified that you never had specific information about Carlos Montilla and that's not why you were there that night, right?"

"I had never seen Carlos Montilla until that night."

After more questioning, LaFontaine was dismissed and returned to his seat at the prosecutor's table, a smile on his grooved face.

Two other police officers testified for the prosecution. Edward Fleming, a barrel-chested black man with a lumbering walk, testified in uniform. A police officer for ten years, Fleming had been undercover for the past three years on the anti-crime unit in Dorchester. That October he was LaFontaine's partner, but his testimony added nothing to the prosecution's case. He could not identify the defendant as the man he observed that evening.

When Blair cross-examined Fleming, he established that the officer had made observations of drug transactions only from the school parking lot and that he did not use binoculars that evening. "We only had one pair of binoculars," Fleming said, "and my partner was using the binoculars."

"So all of your observations were made with your eyes."

"My eyesight."

"With no aid of binoculars."

"No binoculars, no." It was about a hundred yards, he said, between the school parking lot and the apartment building. Fleming contradicted LaFontaine on the time of Montilla's arrest, and he also testified, "I don't remember him telling me that there was three black men in the hallway." (*How could he have forgotten that? I was astounded.*)

Under further questioning, Fleming said again he was too far away to identify the suspect's face; only LaFontaine saw him close enough. What he could see was "a slim-built Hispanic male with curly hair."

"And did he have a particular type haircut?" Blair asked.

"From a distance away I could see curly hair. It was kind of long. Half way."

"But you could see money being changed from that distance?"

"I could see money being exchanged."

Fleming's testimony was interrupted by the luncheon recess, a welcome break from the stuffy courtroom. As usual, I shunned the elevator (and the interminable wait for it) and walked down the eight flights of stairs. Not only was it faster, but going up and down the stairs was good practice for my upcoming trek in Nepal in October. This time, remembering LaFontaine's testimony, I stopped on a landing to look back up. These stairs had risers and you couldn't see through them, but even so I couldn't visualize how LaFontaine could see into the third-floor apartment from the second-floor landing without a periscope or X-ray vision.

Coming back after lunch, I saw Montilla waiting in the hall outside the courtroom with the two men and two women who had accompanied him both days. The younger of the two women, stylishly dressed in a brown suit, seemed to be Montilla's girlfriend. I can't remember exactly when I learned her name was Evelin. Montilla was pacing up and down, talking rapidly, gesturing with his hands the motion of jumping out of a window, shaking his head in disbelief.

Beginning the afternoon session, Fleming resumed the stand, and we learned that LaFontaine had not testified in front of the grand jury that indicted Montilla; Fleming had. Blair then confirmed that in Fleming's testimony before the lunch break he said he could not positively identify Montilla as one of the men he saw outside #223.

"I said he fit — I can't positively ID, no."

"Did you tell the grand jury that it was Carlos Montilla outside?"

"From my personal observation, it looked like it could have been Carlos Montilla. I probably did say it was Carlos Montilla." Fleming had also told the grand jury that they found a couple of IDs and a license that belonged to Montilla, but under Blair's questioning he now testified that the license and other items belonged to Osario; only a pay stub related to Montilla. No, he had not found the pay stub himself.

The prosecution's next witness was Officer Charles Burch, a tall, handsome black man crisply dressed in a short-sleeved uniform. With his partner, he was driving a police wagon the night of October 1st when they received a description over the air of a man wanted in regard to an incident on Geneva Avenue: a slim Hispanic male with a bushy moustache and a Michael Jackson-style hairdo, wearing only underwear and no shirt. Fifteen or twenty minutes later, driving down Geneva Avenue, about a mile away from the project, Burch spotted a male fitting the description. "We saw him almost on the corner of Geneva and Westville in front of a club. He matched the description pretty much, but he was clothed." Burch spoke clearly, in a straightforward manner. He was by far the most articulate of the three officers.

There were three, maybe four other people standing outside the club, he said. The defendant turned around as the wagon passed him, and when the officers returned he was standing alone on the curb. "We stopped him, told him he fit a description of a person wanted. And we wanted to hold him until somebody could ID him."

"Now did the defendant say anything at this time?"

"He acted as though he couldn't speak English, ma'am." There was no conversation, he said. Burch then radioed the car that wanted the suspect, and Officer Fleming came to the scene. He could not positively identify Montilla, so they all went back to the police station.

"And what happened when you came into the station with the defendant, Carlos Montilla?"

"What happened? As I recall, Officer LaFontaine spotted him and said that was the one."

When it was Blair's turn, he elicited much the same testimony and then asked, "Was anybody drinking that was standing outside of the club?"

"No, I don't recall, sir, anybody drinking."

Yes, Burch was present at the station when Officer LaFontaine asked Montilla to empty his pockets, and Blair asked if he observed anything coming out of the defendant's pockets.

"Not really."

Blair repeated the question. "Did you observe anything being taken from the defendant at the police station?"

"All I can remember is probably some change, maybe a comb, personal papers."

Blair pounced on that. "You saw personal papers? What did you see?"

"All I recall seeing is, like personal papers, like you know, papers you would have in your pocket. I don't remember exactly what it was."

"How thick was the stack?"

"Very thin."

"But it was there, right?"

"That's correct," Burch said. (*I thought Blair had made a significant point: Burch contradicted LaFontaine's testimony that Montilla had no personal papers on him.*)

After Burch left the stand, an afternoon recess was announced. It was now three o'clock, and I was grateful to leave the courtroom for a while. The heavy air was beginning to smell like a locker room. Upstairs we had a chance to cool off and stretch our legs. Almost everyone looked glazed from heat and boredom. Most people were quiet, but I chatted again with Ralph. He had noticed that I was taking the stairs rather than the elevator, and I told him about the upcoming trek in Nepal. He asked many questions.

We would be trekking for two weeks in Jugal Himal, I told him, a lesser-known but beautiful area in eastern-central Nepal, with porters to carry all the baggage, a kitchen crew to cook for us, and Sherpas to guide us. The leader was a good friend, an Englishman who lived in Scotland and led walks there and in the Himalayas. I had walked with Andy twice in Scotland and knew he was an excellent, experienced leader. The group of ten was all Brits except for me and one other American woman. Yes, I would give Ralph one of Andy's brochures.

Although I happily answered Ralph's questions, the trek being much on my mind, it felt a bit odd, even frivolous, to be chatting about something so remote from the proceedings that would determine a young man's fate.

After the recess, Blair called the first defense witness. Anna Reyes, dressed in pants and a flowered smock, had a sweet, round face and dark hair slicked back into a neat bun at her neck. She began answering questions in English, but Blair soon requested a translator, which more than doubled the time for each question and answer. She and Montilla were first cousins, Reyes said. The night of October 1st, he came for dinner as he often did, and he left at about six o'clock to go to the Catania Club. He always went to that place, she said. Beland, in cross-examination, confirmed that Montilla came to dinner alone, was there about an hour, and left about six o'clock. Reyes did not go to the club with Montilla or see him later that night. "So actually the only thing you can say is from five to six he ate at your house?" Beland summed up, and Reyes said, "Yes."

The next defense witness was Guillermo Salazar, a middle-aged man in a dark suit, who also testified through the interpreter. Salazar had been at the Catania Social Club for eight years as manager and bartender. Yes, he had seen Carlos Montilla on October 1st, first at the House of Pizza, in the same building as the club, sometime between five and six o'clock. At 6:30 Montilla had come into the club. He sat at the bar, waiting to play pool with somebody, and Salazar served him a beer. From the time he opened the club at about 5:30 until he closed at 1:30, Salazar did not leave the premises. Montilla was wearing the same clothes all evening, Salazar said.

"And is it your testimony that you did not see Carlos Montilla leave the premises at all during the evening?"

"No, until ten at night."

Under Beland's cross examination, Salazar testified that he stayed behind the bar, and the members came to him if they wanted drinks. On a given night there might be up to forty people in the club, sitting at tables, watching TV, or playing pool. Montilla had been a member for four years; he used to go almost every day, but lately he hadn't come in, Salazar told us.

"Now, since Carlos Montilla was coming into the club, he's actually become friends with you, right?"

"Well, like all the other members, for me they're all my friends."

"And in fact, Carlos Montilla asked you to come in to court?"

"Yes. I did him the favor to come in, because I know he was arrested outside because of what my wife told me."

"You didn't see anything that happened outside?"

"No. Only because of what she told me, because they were drinking out there. And she asked the officer, why they were arresting him." He did not actually see Montilla leave the club, but around ten o'clock somebody who thought he might be jealous told him that Montilla was outside talking to his wife. No, his wife was not arrested, just Montilla.

After Salazar left the stand, the judge announced that we were in recess until ten o'clock the next morning. It had been a long day of testimony with much to sort out. How different it was from TV and movies, where there is no waiting, no repetition, no confusion. Dramatic and precise, Hollywood's version was worlds away from the proceedings in the drab courtroom where I was trying my best to find and follow the thread of truth. As I made my way through the maze, I wondered again if I could trust my instincts about Montilla and LaFontaine.

three

ON THURSDAY MORNING, THE THIRD day of the trial, Blair's
first witness was the defendant, Carlos Montilla. On the previous two days he had worn plain short-sleeved shirts and khaki pants, but that day he had on a silky dark-blue leisure suit.
With his dark good looks and gold chain, he could have been a
television actor playing a flashy Latino. Through the interpreter, he identified himself as Carlos Manuel Montilla. His knees
began to jiggle up and down and never stopped throughout his
testimony.

Blair asked him where he was living at the time of his arrest,
and Montilla replied, "10 Hammond Street...Roxbury." On that
date he had gone to his cousin's house in Dorchester, arriving
around four in the afternoon, and had lunch. He then went to
the pizza place next door to the Catania Club, staying there
until Mr. Salazar opened the club. "I used to go to the club
often to play pool every day."

"Now Mr. Montilla, what happened after you got to the
social club?"

"Well, I was playing pool. And I had a beer. All of a sud-
den I felt hot. So I went outside. And when I went outside, the

officer that was here yesterday came over and asked me what my name was. And I told him, my name is Carlos Montilla. And then he told me, you are arrested.

"And I said to him, why? Because — he told me, because you're drinking in public."

"What happened after that?"

"I said, well, okay. And they put me inside the truck."

"Before the truck moved to the police station, did an Officer Fleming come to the truck?"

"I don't remember very well. But somebody like him came over, yes."

Montilla described the scene at the police station: LaFontaine asked him his name and told him to take everything out of his pockets. "He told me that I should give him the wallet." (*But LaFontaine had told the jury Montilla had no wallet or anything else personal on him.*)

"What did he do with it?"

"When I took out the wallet, he started taking out papers, because I always carry lots of addresses and papers in my wallet. At that time, I had that little piece of paper that's over there."

Blair asked for Exhibit 10, showed it to Montilla, and asked if he'd ever seen it before. Montilla, speaking directly to the woman who was translating for him, answered, "Tell him, yes. Because, this, I always had it in my wallet always."

"Is that your pay stub?"

"This is my pay stub when I worked in that company, Guardian Company."

"Are you working now?"

"No. I'm in lay-off. Lay-off."

"Now, moving back to Officer LaFontaine, when he was looking at your papers, did he do anything with the papers?"

Montilla spoke rapidly for several minutes before the interpreter translated: "He started filling out papers. He started writing notes. He took all the papers, paper by paper, from my wallet. He took out everything. Then he did this." Montilla made a motion of pushing something away. "He put it to the side, and he put it underneath other papers. And he told me, take back your wallet, and take down your pants. And he took my underwear and two chains that I had and two rings. And when he gave me back the wallet, he kept this paper," Montilla said, gesturing toward the pay stub. "And I didn't check my wallet because I figure what interest is he going to have in that piece of paper."

"Did he show you any pictures at the police station?"

"Yes. He showed me a picture. One of those pictures are instantaneous. *(I assumed he meant a Polaroid.)* But he never let me look at it in my hands. He only passed it, like this, in front of my face quickly. And he told me that man was me, that I had thrown myself from a third floor. And I said to him, you're crazy. And I don't know. I was laughing. I was laughing. I didn't give it any importance. And he said, that's all right. Continue laughing, because I am gonna make you serve three years in jail. And I didn't give importance to that, because I didn't know what was going on. I didn't give it any importance."

Blair asked, "Did you hear Officer LaFontaine testify yesterday and the day before that he found that exhibit at the apartment at 223 Geneva Avenue?"

"Yes, I heard it. But that's what he says."

"Have you ever been to 223 Geneva Avenue?"

"Never in my life I've lived there. I haven't even visited there."

Blair directed Montilla's attention to the diagram of the project and asked if he had ever been to any of the buildings. "In none of them. I've never been there. Never."

"Is it your testimony that you were at the Catania Social Club from the time you entered to the time you were taken away by Officer Burch?"

"Yes, for sure."

"Did you ever go to the apartment building on that evening, or did you ever distribute or deal any drugs?"

"Never. Never have I visited those apartments."

"Your witness," Blair said to the prosecutor. Beland walked to the microphone and began her cross-examination.

"Sir, where do you live now?"

"In Wellesley," Montilla answered. *(Wellesley? How could he afford to live in that wealthy suburb?)*

Beland asked Montilla where he was living two years ago, at the time of his arrest, and he answered, "10 Hammond Street, Roxbury." How far was that from his cousin Anna's house? Beland asked. It was far, he answered, quite far. No, he didn't have a car at that time; he would take a taxi to his cousin's house. Beland then asked who Montilla was living with.

"With the woman that's over there." Montilla pointed to Evelin, the striking, dark-haired woman who had been with him each day, now sitting in the first row of the spectators' benches. Her face was impassive, almost stony.

"Now, how long had you been living at the Hammond Street apartment?"

"Like, a year and five months. Something like that."

He worked for a year or so at the Guardian Company, but could not remember when he started there. "When I got here to Boston, Massachusetts, I was working there. And then, work got slow. So I went back to Puerto Rico to live. Then I came back again, and I started working there again."

"Okay. So when did you come back from Puerto Rico?"

"Well, tell her, if she wants me to I'll go and look for the papers to check the time when I came back from Puerto Rico. I don't remember that."

"Do you remember what year?"

"No, I don't remember which year. I just know that I came back from Puerto Rico again."

Beland backed up to the month of the arrest and asked if Montilla was working at all then. He answered no, but then added, "A friend of mine that has a restaurant, sometimes I used to go there and help them in the counter. But I always used to carry that little piece of paper in my wallet and with lots of others that I have here."

"Okay, for some reason you held onto this little piece of paper and took it everywhere you went, right?"

"Yes, I used to carry it always, because for anything that came up if somebody asked for some identification, I could show it to somebody."

"Do you have a wallet with you, sir?"

"Tell her since I've been twelve years old, my father taught me to wear a wallet. And I have it here." Montilla reached into his back pocket and pulled out his wallet. He was becoming more and more agitated under Beland's questioning, and his knees jiggled in double time. But my gut feeling was strong and clear: *This nervous young man was telling the truth.*

He showed Beland the ID he now carried; it was not a license but had his picture and address. "I took it out a few days ago," he said. At the time of his arrest, he only had "that piece of paper that's over there."

"So when anyone wanted identification, this is what you produced. No address, no date of birth. But this was your identification, is that right?"

As Beland asked her questions, she would stride toward the stand and then turn on her heel, so that her retreating back was to Montilla as he answered.

Again, Montilla addressed his answer to the translator: "Tell her that I know this is not identification. But it has my name there, Carlos Montilla. And I would show it."

"Now you said they went through a lot of items, went through your wallet and took all the papers, right?"

"No, it wasn't a lot. He took out paper by paper from my wallet."

Beland wheeled to face Montilla. "And out of all them, he picked that little stub to keep?"

"That was the one that most interested him, for sure."

"Now you were booked, and they took your name, your social security number, and things like that at the station, right?"

"*Si. Si.*"

"And you signed that you received your rights and that you received your property, right?" Beland now had the arrest report in her hand.

"Yes, because Mr. LaFontaine was the one that was filling out the papers. And he told me, sign here. And because he is a police officer, I signed."

"Did you tell anyone your address?"

"No. I don't know. This address there is what he puts down. I don't know anything about what he's planning."

"You didn't — and I am pointing to where it says, 'Address, 223 Geneva Avenue.'"

"I never lived in Geneva Avenue. Never in my life."

"You didn't show them any ID at the station that gave you were living in Roxbury at the time though, did you?"

"No, I didn't show him anything. Because he didn't ask me where I lived or anything. He just said to me, lend me your wallet."

"How much was the rent where you were staying over in Roxbury?"

"I don't know, because my girlfriend is in charge of that," Montilla answered, his knees pumping up and down, his eyes on the floor.

"Okay. So what did you use for money? You weren't working."

"Oh, yes, I was working. Because I was helping my friend in the Restaurant LaQuanita." The restaurant was in Dorchester, on Geneva Avenue.

"Now what time were you working when you were working there?"

"No, I didn't say I was working. I said that I was helping him out, and he gave me money."

"Well, when did you do that?"

Montilla looked toward LaFontaine at the prosecutor's table. "After this man invented the story he is inventing."

Beland widened her eyes. "Excuse me."

"After this story that this man is inventing. Because I don't know what he has against me." *My skin felt cold as I heard those words.*

Beland now stood at the microphone so that the jury could clearly see her disdain for the young man in the witness chair. "That's when you started working at this place getting money where you didn't really work and you just helped out?"

"I helped the man with everything that needed to be done. I would do it."

"At night?"

"No, during the day."

"And that's how you got your money to take taxis back and forth from Roxbury to Dorchester every night when you were hanging out at the Catania Club, is that right?"

"No, tell her that in the club there's a lot of members, and some of them have cars. And sometimes they would give me rides. Or other times I would take a taxi."

"Well, how would you get to your cousin's where you ate almost every night?"

"In taxi and in train."

"Your girlfriend didn't make dinner for you every night, huh?"

"She cooked but she cooked differently than my cousin. Because it's a different flavor." Montilla was slumped down in the witness chair, his head turned to the side.

"Now you had a fifty-dollar bill when you were arrested, right?"

"No, I had ninety dollars."

"You had ninety dollars when you were arrested?"

"Ninety dollars. And I remember because I wasn't drunk."

"Well, where did you get the ninety dollars? You weren't working."

"What that I wasn't working? I was helping out my friend in the restaurant. I was helping out."

Beland rolled her big eyes as the interpreter translated that answer. Then she changed the subject and asked who Montilla was with outside the club when Officer Burch approached him.

"With Mr. Salazar's wife."

"No one else?"

"Maybe there was another person. I think there was another person outside, but I didn't know who he was."

"But when the officer swung back around in the wagon, you were by yourself then, right?"

"No, I was with Mr. Salazar's wife. Because she asked, why are you arresting him? Because he asked me my name. And I said, Carlos Montilla, to the officer. And then Mr. Salazar's wife asked, why are you arresting him? And then the officer said, because he's drinking in public. And because he said so, I just went inside the truck."

"And this is the officer, or at least his partner, who said that you were alone outside the club, not drinking, when he asked you to come to the wagon?"

"Well, that's what he says. But I was with a beer in my hand. And that's what he told me, that it was because I was drinking outside."

"You didn't tell him you couldn't speak English. So there was no conversation?"

"Yes, I told him that I didn't know how to speak English. But Mr. Salazar's wife knows how to speak good English, because she was born here.... She is the one that said, why are you arresting him? And the officer said, because he's drinking in public. And nothing else was spoken. And they just took me."

"Now when you go back and forth from Roxbury to Dorchester, I assume you have keys to the apartment."

"Oh, for sure."

"Well, didn't you have any keys when you were arrested?"

"I don't remember if I had keys. Because sometimes I would take the keys, and sometimes I would leave them."

"Well, look at the booking sheet where you signed for your property. That can be translated if necessary."

Montilla bent his head close to the interpreter as she read to him from the booking sheet, and after a few minutes of talk, the translator looked at Beland and said, "Well, tell her that I have my chain and my watch, like any other person that has a chain and a watch."

"Right. No keys."

"I don't know."

"No wallet."

"Yes, of that I'm sure, that I had a wallet."

Beland took back the sheet and read, "It says, ring, man's ring, gold watch not taken. Held for evidence, fifty dollars."

"Yes, but tell her that Mr. LaFontaine gave me back my wallet."

"In fact, you were sitting here when Officer LaFontaine said you didn't have any identification at the station, right?"

"Yes, that's right. But that's what he says. All I know is that I always have a wallet ever since I was twelve years old."

"And you've never been up Geneva Avenue?"

"Never in my life. But I have been in Geneva Avenue, but not near the projects. No. Because they were charging me that I threw myself from a third floor."

"And you wouldn't do that?" Beland asked, her tone more and more sarcastic.

"Oh, but if I throw myself from a third floor, I break both my legs. And the second day I went to the court, the second day after they arrested me, I went into the court walking well."

"You didn't go down any stairs from the roof did you, so you wouldn't get hurt?"

"Tell her, what stairs. Because I don't know what stairs." Montilla looked confused and very agitated.

"Now, your hair was a little bit longer back then, right?"

"No, my hair all my life I've had it like this. Maybe a little bit longer, but always moist."

Beland pursued that. "A little bit wet? Little ringlets?"

"No. Wet. Just wet. So my hair is soft so I can comb it. Not like Michael Jackson."

"Not longer?"

"I am not Michael Jackson!"

"I don't think that's an issue," Beland replied, almost sneering.

When she finished her questioning, Blair stood up and asked, "Mr. Montilla, did you ever tell Officer LaFontaine that your address was 223 Geneva Avenue?"

"Never in my life."

Blair then showed Montilla the booking sheet and asked if his writing was on it.

"Yes. It's down here. I see my name. Because Mr. LaFontaine told me to sign right here. And I put my name."

"Mr. Montilla, where it says in box number 12 the address of 223 Geneva Avenue, is that your handwriting?"

"No, that's not my handwriting."

"Thank you." Blair sat down, Beland said "I have nothing further," and the judge told Carlos, "All right. You may step down."

Montilla did not look at the jury as he left the witness chair. His face, particularly his nose, glistened with sweat. He sat down alone at the defendant's table, as his attorney stood at the microphone ready to question the next witness, who was being sworn in with the help of the interpreter. I stared at Carlos until he turned his head. He met my gaze squarely, but his eyes were full of distress. Then I turned my attention to the witness stand.

Hortensia Nunez, a good friend of Montilla's cousin Anna, had a serene and dignified manner. She lived in the Geneva Avenue project, at #227 directly across from #223. At the time of the incident she was not working and spent considerable time in her apartment. She had never seen Carlos Montilla at the Geneva Avenue apartments. From church she knew the couple, Gonzalo and Maria, who lived on the third floor of #223. Maria had a brother named Pablo who stayed behind when the couple moved to Puerto Rico. She did not know Pablo's last name. She was away at church the evening of October 1, but when she returned she saw the police officers there.

Beland, in cross, confirmed that Nunez was not home the evening of the incident and then asked, "So you can't tell us if Carlos Montilla was there or if Carlos Montilla was not there?"

"Never have I seen him in the Geneva, is what I said. I know all the people."

At the morning recess, cooling off in the jurors' room with the noisy air conditioner cranked up as high as it would go, I stood next to Dorothy, the young mother with deep frown lines. "I think he lives there," she said to me, out of the blue.

"What?" I was surprised out of my own thoughts.

"I think Carlos lives at 223 Geneva Avenue," she repeated. "Because he didn't know his address."

"But at the time of the incident he was living in Roxbury with his girlfriend. I'm sure he said the address. And now they live in Wellesley."

"No," Dorothy shook her head emphatically. "He didn't know his address."

Her certainty made me doubt my own memory. I doubted myself even more after I heard the next defense witness.

Rudy Muchuca, the other alibi witness for Montilla, was a disaster for the defense. His testimony, also through the interpreter, began well enough under Blair's questioning. Yes, he knew Carlos Montilla, and he had seen him on October 1st two years ago at the Catania Club from six o'clock on. They played one game of pool, and Muchuca saw Montilla playing with others. No, he did not leave the club all evening until midnight, and no, neither did Montilla until he went outside and was arrested. Muchuca was certain of it.

Blair then walked into a trap of his own making. He asked Muchuca if he knew any member of the club named Pablo Osario. When Muchuca answered yes, Blair looked startled and asked again, "Do you know that Pablo Osario was a member of the club?"

"Yes."

"He's a member of the Catania Social Club?"

"Yes."

Blair dropped that line of questioning like a hot potato and asked Muchuca about his conversations with Montilla that night, establishing that they had been talking throughout the evening.

When Blair finished, Muchuca was fair game for Beland. She quickly established that Muchuca lived on a street that was between the Geneva Avenue Apartments and the Catania Club, about three blocks from the club. *(So that's where Montilla could have run in his underwear and gotten the clothes he was wearing when he was picked up at the club.)* Then she confirmed that Pablo Osario was a member of the club and that he and Montilla had at least been in each other's presence there.

"Now on October 1st, did you see the defendant at your house?" Yes, he had, around four o'clock.

"And what did you do at the house?"

"In my house?"

"Yes, did you chat? Did you just talk?"

Muchuca paused before answering, then seemed inspired. "We were cooking."

Again, Beland rolled her eyes. "What were *you* cooking?"

"Rice and meat and beans." Yes, they ate dinner there and then went outside to get some air, where they stayed for about twenty minutes.

"And then what did you do after you got some fresh air?"

"Well, we each went to walk around. And I went to do some errands that I had to do."

"So at that point you and Carlos Montilla split up?"

"Yes."

"And when was the next time you saw Carlos Montilla?"

"Well, like the next day."

Blair jumped to his feet. "Your Honor, I think it is appropriate to ask whether or not the witness is informed of the day that he is talking about."

"All right," the judge agreed.

Beland, at the microphone, asked Muchuca if he was talking about October 1st two years ago, and he answered, "Yes."

"Okay. And then it was that same October 1st that you went outside, stayed for some air, and went your separate directions?"

"Yes."

"And the next time you saw him was the next day?"

"Yes."

"And did you hear he was arrested?"

"Yes, they told me."

"You didn't see him, though?"

"No."

To drive her point home, Beland asked Muchuca again, "You weren't there when he got arrested?" But to her obvious surprise, he answered, "Yes." He had thrown her a curve too.

"You were there?" she repeated.

"Inside the club," Muchuca said.

"You were inside the club?"

"Inside the club."

"And you heard Carlos Montilla was arrested outside the club?"

"They told me."

"Thank you, sir. I have nothing further."

Blair sat silently at the defendant's table as the witness was excused.

We were told that there were no more witnesses. Beland entered into evidence the map of the Geneva Avenue project and the defendant's mug shot, which was passed around the jury box. I stared at the face that had grown familiar over the last three days, the eyes as bewildered as in real life. The surprise was the hair. It was curly and tousled, but rather short, with no ringlets. How could that be described as a Michael Jackson hairdo?

On my way back to the courthouse after the lunch recess, I saw Montilla and his girlfriend sitting together on one of the concrete planters for the small trees that shaded the courthouse plaza. (Montilla was out on bail, not in custody.) LaFontaine stood in front of them, talking. Two weeks later, from Blair, I learned what LaFontaine was saying.

"Things are not going well for you," LaFontaine told Montilla in Spanish. *"You are going to go to prison. If I were you, I would run away now."*

Back in the jury room at two o'clock, I waited with the others to be summoned by the court officer. No one said anything until Ralph broke the silence. "Wasn't that a silk suit Carlos was wearing?"

Curt responded, "It looked like it to me."

Janice, the editor, turned to me and said, "I thought it was polyester," and we laughed quietly together.

"And his girlfriend's carrying a Gucci bag," Ralph added. I hadn't noticed her handbag, just that she was stylishly dressed.

"Yeah, the guy's not working, but he lives in Wellesley and wears gold chains," Vincent observed.

Ralph then told us that he too had seen LaFontaine talking to Montilla and his girlfriend at lunch time, outside in front of the courthouse. "I didn't think they were supposed to talk to each other. Makes you wonder what's going on."

At 2:30, the court officer still hadn't come for us, and Vincent said that if we didn't finish today, he'd have to get excused because of his rafting trip. Finally, at about 2:45, the court officer came for us, and we returned to the courtroom. As we filed in, I noticed immediately that no one was sitting at the defendant's table; it was completely bare. Beland was alone at the prosecutor's table. After we sat down in the jury box, she looked over at us and widened her eyes as if seeking sympathy. The judge announced that due to the late hour, we would not hear closing arguments and begin deliberations until tomorrow at ten o'clock. We were dismissed until then.

Ralph and I were chatting on the plaza outside when Vincent caught up with us. "I got excused, but I want to know what happens." He wrote his phone number on a piece of paper and handed it to Ralph, who said, "Why don't you write down your verdict, and I'll look at it after the trial's over. We'll see if you're right."

"Guilty," said Vincent, without ceremony. "Guilty as hell."

"Right," Ralph agreed. I was a little surprised that they didn't ask me what I thought, but I kept quiet.

Surely not everyone believed LaFontaine's testimony? I had confidence in Aaron, Janice, and Cassie, although none of them had said anything to reveal their thoughts about the trial.

That night I took a bold step. I wanted to confirm my commonsense rejection of LaFontaine's statements that only the FBI can remove fingerprints and that he couldn't have had the gun or drug packets fingerprinted even if he had wanted to. I knew a police officer who used to live on Beacon Hill, now teaching at the police academy, and I called him at home. Never mentioning the trial, I told him I wanted to ask him some theoretical questions about fingerprinting.

"You've been robbed," he immediately assumed.

"No, no. This is purely theoretical, to resolve an argument."

Jay gave me a quick education. The Boston Police Department had one fingerprint unit, at District 4 on Berkeley Street, the police headquarters. It was not routine to fingerprint except for major crimes. Or, he gave me an example, when the police enter a room where drugs are found, and everyone says, "Hey, those aren't my drugs."

"What if a suspect fled the scene and left a gun behind?" I asked.

Jay laughed. "You don't let that happen. You cover the rear."

"But assuming it does happen?"

"You would want to print the gun," he said emphatically. "But sometimes there's a problem if an idiot cop who doesn't know any better picks up the gun and smudges the only prints." Just like LaFontaine!

Then I asked the $64,000 question. "What if someone told you only the FBI can remove fingerprints?"

His answer was music to my ears. "That's hogwash. You can take prints from almost anything except rough surfaces like brick or concrete. Paper and tinfoil are very easy."

Jubilant, I thanked him profusely and copied over my scrawled notes onto yellow notepaper. I folded the sheet in half and put it in my handbag to take with me tomorrow. I knew what I had done was probably irregular, even though I never mentioned my real reason for calling. But hadn't Henry Fonda in *Twelve Angry Men* bought a duplicate of the switchblade murder weapon?

I was glad to be armed with my yellow sheet of notes, even though I was certain that, unlike Fonda, I wouldn't be the only one who had doubts about the defendant's guilt.

four

THE NEXT MORNING I MADE the now-familiar journey to the courthouse, a steamy walk up Beacon Street, past the gold-domed State House on the left, the brownstone Athenaeum library on the right, and then left behind the One Beacon Street skyscraper, where granite steps led down to the courthouse plaza; through the glass doors of the monolith courthouse, past the security personnel who now recognized me as a juror and waved me on, and then the solitary climb up the stairs to the eighth floor, past the courtroom to the special staircase up to the jury room.

It had quickly become routine, this journey, as if it were my only life. The bookstore, where I had been for ten years, seemed faraway and unreal, but I knew as soon as the jury duty was over, I would slide back into my normal life without a ripple. Or so I thought.

That Friday morning as I walked past the courtroom, I turned my head to look at Carlos Montilla, who was sitting on the bench to the right of the door, his head resting on his girlfriend's shoulder. He spoke to her in Spanish as I went by, words that I would not have understood even if I had heard them. A few weeks later, I learned what he had said.

"*That woman keeps staring at me. I think she wants me to go to jail.*"

The morning session in the courtroom was interrupted after only half an hour, and a recess was suddenly called. When we came back after a few minutes and resumed our seats, Judge Steele emerged from his chambers in his shirtsleeves. His non-judicial attire was both casual and alarming, as was the announcement he made. There had been a bomb scare. Usually there was nothing to these things, he reassured us, but we could decide whether we wanted to leave.

Silence in the jury box and then I spoke up, "I vote to stay."

Cassie gave me a look of alarm but said nothing. No one else said anything either that I recall. Steele returned to his chambers and after a few moments appeared again fully robed. It was in that uneasy atmosphere, half listening for an explosion, that we heard the final witness for the defense.

Nelida Salazar, wife of the Catania Club manager, was a last-minute witness. An attractive dark-haired woman, she too testified through the interpreter, although Montilla had said she could speak good English. Blair established that she had been at the Catania Club on October 1st and had seen Montilla there.

"What time of day did you see Mr. Montilla there?"

"At night, around 8:30. I got to the club at 8:30."

"When did you leave the club?"

"Around one in the morning." Mrs. Salazar spoke without hesitation, in a clear, composed voice. Yes, at one point in the evening she went outside with Mr. Montilla. "We were talking outside, and I was drinking a beer in a glass, and he had a beer."

"And did something happen when you were outside drinking your beer?"

"Yes. The police came by in a police wagon. Then he stopped. He came out and he arrested him."

"Was there any conversation between the police officer and yourself that evening?"

"Well, I asked the police officer why he was taking him away."

"And what did he respond?"

"Because he was drinking in public."

"And do you know which officer that was?"

"Fleming," she answered.

"And did he have any conversation, Officer Fleming, with Carlos Montilla?"

"Well, he asked him what his name was and where he lived. And he told him. And he took him away. And I asked him why he was taking him away. And he said, for drinking in public. And he told me, you want to also go? And I told him, no. So I went inside because they were taking him away."

It was Beland's turn. "A couple of questions, ma'am. When were you asked to come in here?"

"Well, I came in out of my own will, because what they are saying about him, that's not true."

"Now, how long were you outside with Carlos Montilla?"

"Like, half an hour. I went outside, like, around 10:30, and around 11:05 is when they arrested him."

"Now, you say Fleming came up, got out of the wagon, stopped and arrested Carlos Montilla for drinking in public?"

"Yes."

"No one told you the name Fleming, that Fleming was involved in the case, huh?"

"No. Tell her that I know Detective Fleming very well, and he knows me." Mrs. Salazar said this quite firmly.

Beland cast doubt on her version of the arrest — it differed from that of Fleming and Burch — but she left unchallenged her statement that Carlos was at the club when she arrived at 8:30, when the suspect was allegedly dealing drugs a mile away.

As Blair began his closing arguments, I strained to hear his soft voice. Only LaFontaine identified Montilla, he said, and LaFontaine was lying. LaFontaine did not want us to believe Montilla had any papers on him, but the government's own witness, the uniformed police officer, contradicted him. That was important, Blair told us, because LaFontaine said the pay stub was found in the house, while Montilla said LaFontaine took it from him at the police station. The pay stub was the only evidence besides LaFontaine's observations.

"I suggest to you that he fabricated that," Blair said. "That's not true, but he will do anything at all. They are a team — our government is a team here, including the assistant district attorney. They've got resources."

Beland looked over to the jury box and rolled her eyes.

Blair gestured toward Carlos, who was watching him intently as the interpreter translated into his ear. "You are his only resource. There is nothing between him and prison except you right now."

Beland shot up from her seat. "Objection, Your Honor."

"Sustained. Stricken. That is stricken, Mr. Foreman, and ladies and gentlemen, the reference to prison."

Blair, beginning to look wilted and almost desperate, walked closer to the jury box. "I'm suggesting to you we've got a one-on-one situation. We've got LaFontaine versus the defendant. He wants this man, and he wants this man to be convicted."

After a brief mention of the three alibi witnesses, Blair wound up his argument with a final attack on LaFontaine, accusing him again of taking the pay stub out of Montilla's wallet. Any police officer who would do that would stop at nothing. "He would tell you anything at all. This is part of his little package to put him away on this charge."

Beland stood up by her chair and faced the jury box. With disdain in her voice, she began her closing arguments. "Ladies and gentlemen, after listening to Mr. Blair, I get the impression Mr. Blair wants everyone to believe that the government is out at this stage to get Carlos Montilla, that the police are lying, a conspiracy to get this individual." She told us that the only reason the defendant was before us was because he was in the drug business that night, selling drugs out of 223 Geneva Avenue.

She reviewed some of the facts and reaffirmed the value of Fleming's testimony. "He saw drug transactions. He saw an individual looking like Montilla. He just can't tell you positively." Not only was there possession of drugs, there was intent to distribute, Beland asserted. The drugs were packaged in tinfoil and plastic bags ready for customers.

As for Blair's argument that Montilla had an alibi, there was no credible evidence for that. "I suggest the defendant told you a story, and he brought in a group of people to tell you a story. Even their stories weren't straight." In her remarks about Montilla's alibi, Beland made no reference to the Salazars. What we had heard from the defense, she assured us, was a story. Nothing was credible, nothing was truthful.

"Just weigh all the evidence carefully," she said. "When you do that, based on the facts, you will be able to say, Yes, the defendant is guilty of trafficking." It was trafficking, she said, because of possession of more than twenty-eight grams of cocaine, as the analysis would tell us.

"The gun? The gun was in the defendant's hand. The gun was pointed at the officer who was, I think he said, about four feet away. He had the close-up. He saw the gun. He saw the defendant's face close up a short distance away. He was the one who was there." Beland left us with a vivid image: a gun-wielding Montilla face to face with LaFontaine.

The judge then gave his instructions to the jury, long, detailed, impossible to absorb in full. We were the final judges of the facts and the credibility of the witnesses, he told us. We must base our verdicts on evidence presented in the courtroom, nothing else. Unlike English judges, he said, judges in Massachusetts were forbidden by statute to comment on the evidence. "This is to drive home the fact that you jurors are the final judges of facts in trials, especially in criminal cases."

He reminded us that the defendant comes into court presumed to be innocent. "This presumption of innocence is a rule of law that compels you to find the defendant innocent in absence of evidence that convinces you as reasonable individuals that the defendant is guilty beyond a reasonable doubt." It was not easy, he said, to define reasonable doubt. It was not just possible doubt, because anything in human affairs is open to some doubt. Reasonable doubt was if jurors did not feel "an abiding conviction to a moral certainty of the truth of the charges."

The accused is entitled to the benefit of the doubt. All presumptions of law are in favor of innocence. It was not sufficient if the charge was shown to be probably true; the evidence must establish the truth of a fact to a reasonable and moral certainty. We were the final judges of the credibility of witnesses. He explained that is why courtrooms are designed so that the jury is close to the witness stand, to allow us to draw upon our observations, our own life experience and knowledge of human nature, in rendering judgment.

Our verdict must be unanimous. All jurors must agree either guilty or not guilty.

After the judge finished, the clerk told us that the panel of thirteen jurors would be reduced to twelve. In front of him was a small wooden drum. "I have placed the names of all of the jurors in the barrel except for the foreman, and one juror's name will be drawn. That juror will be designated as an alternate juror." *Not me,* I prayed, as the clerk spun the cylinder, opened its hatch, and reached inside. He read from the slip and announced Ruth's name. She would be separated from the rest of us during deliberations, but must remain in attendance until the trial was over.

At 10:50 a.m. the clerk announced, "The jury may retire to deliberate," and we filed upstairs. I walked into the jury room with the others, and the door closed behind us.

five

SILENTLY, WE CONVERGED ON THE wooden table in the middle of the dingy, fluorescent-lit room. Chairs slid noiselessly on the tweedy carpeting as we chose seats and settled in. Aaron, the foreman, took a chair at the head, draping his suit jacket around the back of his chair and rolling up his sleeves. I sat to his left, on the side of the table closest to the door. The air conditioner thumped away at its highest setting; someone turned it down a notch. The court officer laid on the table the exhibits entered into evidence. He handed the foreman a stack of verdict slips and told us that he would be outside the locked door; we could knock if we needed anything. There was a bathroom within the jury room, off to the right. Lunch would be brought to us about one o'clock.

We inspected the exhibits for a few minutes, passing them back and forth: packets of cocaine and marijuana; a police envelope containing $940; a Smith and Wesson .38 and the bullets removed from it; incident and arrest reports; a map of the housing project; Montilla's pay stub, his mug shot, and the red underwear taken from him at the time of arrest. I took the pay stub and studied it, a thin piece of paper that had been folded small. On the back the name "Evelin" was written in childish printing, followed by a phone number.

Aaron, an accountant who had been on a jury before and had testified twice as an expert witness in other trials, deftly took charge after we finished looking at the exhibits. "Before we take a vote, let's go around the table and tell our reactions. I'll begin," he said. "I thought all the prosecution witnesses were credible, and none of the defense witnesses were." I couldn't believe my ears: *All* of the prosecution witnesses, *none* of the defense witnesses? "I think the contradictions in the officers' testimony are reasonable and understandable and proof that it wasn't a conspiracy as the defense attorney alleged." Aaron went on to explain why he thought the defendant was guilty, but I can remember only his stunning opening words.

Ralph, who sat opposite me on Aaron's right, spoke next. He agreed with Aaron, as I expected he would, and added, "LaFontaine's been on the force for sixteen years. If he weren't a good honest cop, we would have heard testimony about suspensions and so forth."

It was not my turn, but I interjected, "We can't assume that."

Ralph defended himself. "Well, it's true. If there was anything irregular about him, we would have heard about it." Several of the others spoke out to agree with Ralph.

Curt was next. He repeated what Aaron and Ralph had said and added, "You can't believe any of the defense witnesses. They're his relatives and friends, and they just want to help him. And what was a guy without a job doing with a fifty-dollar bill in his pocket? I never carry a fifty."

My sinking heart lifted as Cassie, the soft-spoken teacher who lived in Dorchester where the alleged crimes had taken place, said, "I have mixed feelings; I'm not sure. I know that when drug deals were happening on my street, it turned out the cops were in on it."

Joey, looking both bored and angry, recited the names of the three police witnesses: "LaFontaine saw him, Fleming saw him, Burch saw him. He's guilty." (Had Joey listened at all to the testimony? Burch hadn't been anywhere near the scene.)

Janice, whom I had expected to share my views, shook her head sadly. "I wanted to believe he was innocent, but the prosecutor convinced me that he was guilty."

Dorothy said simply, "I agree with the others. He's guilty."

Guilty, guilty, guilty — all around the table until we got to blonde Tricia, who was sitting next to me. "I also have mixed feelings," she announced, blessedly. "I was really surprised when I saw the mug shot yesterday. After all that talk about a Michael Jackson hairdo, I expected long ringlets. But he doesn't have a Michael Jackson hairdo at all — it's much too short."

Ralph pointed to the mug shot on the table. "Well, that's *my* idea of a Michael Jackson hairdo."

"But I have the *Thriller* album at home," Tricia protested, "and Michael Jackson's hair is completely different."

I was the last person to speak. Would it have been any different if I had gone first? "I am not convinced that Carlos Montilla has been proven guilty. There is very little evidence. It all rests on LaFontaine's testimony, and I didn't find him credible. He seems to have a bad memory, and I don't trust his identification. I think this could well be a case of mistaken identity. I know that eyewitness identifications can be tricky. I remember this case in Texas —"

"Irrelevant!" Joey shouted from the other end of the table. "Immaterial!" He had obviously watched many courtroom dramas on television.

"Why don't you believe him?" Curt, too, raised his voice.

"Let her talk," Aaron said, "so we can finish with this."

I went on, still optimistic. In groups I often emerged as the leader and could usually persuade others to my point of view. "I did find some of the defense witnesses credible. For instance, I thought Mrs. Salazar was very believable. She was clear about the time, and she backed up Carlos's alibi."

"But she was brought in at the last minute," Esther, the black woman, said. "And they told us she spoke good English but she didn't."

"I don't think it should matter to us when she was brought in," I replied. "We should look at her testimony on its own merits. And I believed her."

"But LaFontaine saw him," Ralph said. "And he identified the red underwear. It was the same that he saw on the guy with the gun."

The orangey-red bikini underwear sat in its Ziploc bag on the table. Tricia pointed to it and said, "I used to work in a clothing store, and I sold underwear like that all the time to the Hispanic men."

Mildred, the grandmotherly woman, chimed in. "Yes, they all wear that kind of underwear." (How did she know this? I never found out.)

I brought up another point. "If Carlos did jump out a window in his underwear and went somewhere where he found clothes and money, why wouldn't he stay there? It was safe. Why would he be standing calmly on a street corner and not run away when he saw the police?"

Ralph had an answer. "He knew he had arranged his alibi, so he could act real cool."

"How could that nervous young man on the stand act 'real cool' in that situation? It just doesn't fit," I said.

"But LaFontaine identified him," Curt said. "Why don't you believe him?"

I tried to explain how bothered I was by LaFontaine's evasiveness about time, especially on the incident and arrest reports.

"You're just dwelling on little things, like the defense attorney did," Dorothy said. "I thought he was going to bore us to death."

"But little things can be crucial. These are serious charges, and Carlos can go to prison for at least three years if we convict him."

"Now you've shown your true colors," Aaron said in disgust. "You just feel sorry for him."

"But I don't just feel sorry for him," I protested. "I don't think there's enough evidence to prove him guilty. Why are we looking at that flimsy little pay stub instead of fingerprint evidence?"

"That's a good question," Cassie said. "Why didn't they fingerprint the gun and the drug packets?"

"I wondered that too," Janice said, and several others echoed her.

"LaFontaine told us they wouldn't let him do that," Ralph volunteered.

Here was my opening. "And he also told us only the FBI can remove fingerprints —"

Aaron interrupted me. "But he said that about the pay stub,

not the gun or the drugs." Aaron had listened closely to the testimony and remembered it well, often better than I did.

"In any case I happened to know that what LaFontaine told us is not true," I said. "Last night I talked to a police officer I know, and he gave me the real story about fingerprinting."

Aaron was furious. "That is totally out of line and improper. You never should have talked to someone outside, and we can't even consider what he told you." (He was correct, of course, and I could have been dismissed if he had chosen to tell the judge.)

I defended myself. "I said nothing about the trial. It was a purely theoretical discussion. He told me it's not routine to fingerprint except for a major crime, but if a suspect fled the scene and left a gun behind, they would want to print it. And he said it's hogwash that only the FBI can lift fingerprints. You can get prints from almost anything except rough surfaces, and paper or tinfoil is very easy."

"We can't take any of this information into account," Aaron instructed the others. "It was up to the defense attorney to present it as evidence."

"So we had some sloppy police work," Curt shrugged. "There's still enough evidence as far as I'm concerned."

"It's not enough for me," I said. "It all goes back to LaFontaine —"

"Why don't you believe him?" Several of them were shouting at once.

When I tried to answer, they shouted, "You're dwelling on little things."

We had been wrangling for about an hour when Cassie said in her quiet voice, "I've now realized that someone has to be lying, and I don't think it was the police officers. I've changed my mind, and I'm ready to vote to convict."

Tricia followed suit. "I am too."

Cassie looked at me and said, "I think you should change your mind too."

I was alone.

They all stared at me, waiting, their stony faces willing me to surrender. Never before had I felt the force of a group against me. I was used to affection and respect, not just from friends but from strangers too.

Now I sat alone, the target of eleven hard stares and eleven opposing wills. Seconds ticked by on the round schoolroom-like clock on the wall. I shook my head. "I'm sorry. I know you all want to get this over with, but I have too many doubts. I can't do it."

Frustrated and disgusted, the others began again. "LaFontaine saw him. Why don't you believe him? Why do you dwell on the details?" If I tried to answer, I was interrupted. Often three or four people were shouting at me at once. "Please," I begged, "can you just talk one at a time?" My heart was pounding. I felt as if I were on trial too, and like Carlos, I could only be guilty: guilty of just feeling sorry for him, guilty of being unreasonable, guilty of not bowing to the majority.

A knock on the door at one o'clock brought reprieve. The court officer announced that lunch was ready. We all stood up and followed him to an empty jurors' room down the hall. A cold lunch was laid out on the table there: coleslaw and potato salad — made mostly of mayonnaise — tuna salad, cheese and cold cuts, white bread, lukewarm cans of soda. My stomach was knotted tight, and I could eat only a few bites.

This jurors' room, also barely air-conditioned, had at least not been heated up by twelve tense bodies, and we had a chance to cool off, both physically and mentally. I drank one can of soda quickly and took another back to the deliberation room. Everyone seemed calmer as we resumed our seats around the table. Maybe now I could collect my thoughts, maybe now I could speak without being interrupted, maybe now they would listen to what I had to say.

I began again with LaFontaine's evasiveness about time. Reaching out to the arrest report in front of me, I knocked over the soda. Horrified, I watched the dark fluid spread over the sheet. Oh, great, I thought. Now I've destroyed evidence. I grabbed some napkins, and Tricia helped me blot up the liquid. Amazingly, the sheet survived with no sign of its dunking.

Aaron offered a reason for LaFontaine's evasiveness. "Maybe he doesn't want to be pinned down to a particular time. That way Carlos can't make up an alibi."

"But why doesn't he just tell the truth?" I responded. Aaron did not answer, and I was still too shaken by the soda fiasco to press him.

I tried another approach. "I don't think the defense witnesses should be dismissed so easily. Rudy Muchuca was a disaster, of course, but both Mr. and Mrs. Salazar were credible and Hortensia Nunez too."

"But Mrs. Salazar said Carlos was arrested for drinking in public and that contradicts what Burch told us," Aaron said.

"Perhaps there was a genuine misunderstanding. I think we have to make some allowances for the language barrier. Things can get confused in translation."

Ralph said, "I know a little Spanish, and when they said *bueno*, the interpreter translated *well*."

Tricia backed me up. "But there's a completely different word order in Spanish."

"Why don't they speak English?" Ralph said. "They live here."

"Anyway," Aaron went on, "Burch was sure that Carlos wasn't arrested for drinking in public. And I thought Burch was the most credible of the three officers." Burch was the officer who, driving by, had seen Carlos standing outside the club and thought he fit the suspect's description that had gone out over the air.

"But Burch was the least important of the prosecution witnesses," I said. "Where does that leave LaFontaine?"

"I thought LaFontaine was credible too," Aaron said coldly. "I just thought Burch presented himself very well."

"I agree. But Burch contradicted LaFontaine about Carlos having personal papers in his pocket. Do you believe him or LaFontaine?"

Esther answered. "It could've been the fifty-dollar bill folded up that Burch saw."

"Do you really think Burch would mistake a fifty-dollar bill for personal papers?" I asked her.

"He could've," she answered.

Aaron spoke up again. "We're going to do a test." He ripped into three pieces a sheet of the pale-green computer paper that had been given us for notes. "Here," he said, handing one piece to me and the others to Ralph and Curt. "Write down how much time has passed since the lunch break." After we handed the slips back to him, Aaron smiled with satisfaction at the three very different answers, all incorrect. "See?" he said to me. "It's hard to tell how much time has gone by. Just because LaFontaine can't remember is not that significant."

"But it is significant to me," I said. "First of all, he was very evasive when the defense attorney cross-examined him, and that makes me think he's hiding something. And if he has such a poor memory about time, how can he remember details like the black lines on the underwear that he only saw for a few seconds?"

A chorus answered me: "Why do you keep dwelling on little things?"

We were just going around in circles, and I was too exhausted to keep it up. My dry mouth tasted bitter; my face burned. "I think it's time to tell the judge that we're deadlocked. I'm not going to change my vote."

Joey threw his arms into the air, exclaiming "Can you believe this?" Others sighed, clicked their tongues, muttered oaths. Aaron, looking very put-upon, wrote a note to the judge on a torn-off piece of computer paper and read it aloud to us. "One juror is adamantly entrenched in an opposing view" is the phrase I remember. He added, "We don't want to tell them which way we are deadlocked, or the defense attorney will keep us here forever." He went to the door, knocked, and handed the folded note to the court officer outside.

The hot room seemed to be shrinking, and the other jurors felt uncomfortably close to me. I looked away from them and out one of the grimy windows. From this angle, I could glimpse only the stone facade of a nearby building. Then my eyes focused on the exhibits on the tabletop: the packets of drugs, the gun and bullets, the red underwear. They were like the offerings of a bizarre banquet, and the wilted and tense jurors around the table were the unhappy guests, their faces flushed with heat and frustration.

"Why are you being so unreasonable?" Ralph asked me. "What makes you so sure you're right?"

I answered wearily. "I'm not sure I'm right. I may well be wrong. But what I know for certain is that I cannot in good conscience vote guilty when I have so many doubts. I couldn't live with myself if I did."

"You're being too emotional," Curt said. "You just feel sorry for him."

"I can assure you that if I just felt sorry for him, I would have given up hours ago instead of going through this."

The court officer returned and told us, "The judge says you're to keep on deliberating."

The circular battle began again. Most of the time I was being shouted at, and there is much I cannot remember, but some scenes and dialogue come back vividly.

Ralph: "If there weren't something to it, it never would have gotten this far. Where there's smoke, there's fire."

x

Joey, shouting: "LaFontaine saw him, Fleming saw him, Burch saw him! Look at the facts!"

Me: "But only LaFontaine identified him. Fleming made it very clear that he couldn't identify Carlos; he said it over and over. And Burch just thought Carlos fit the suspect's description that went out over the air. He didn't even witness the incident at the project, so —"

Joey, again: "LaFontaine saw him, Fleming saw him, Burch saw him."

x

Me, my head on my hand: "I wouldn't want to be convicted because I happened to be wearing red underwear. There's just not enough evidence."

Curt: "All the evidence you need is right here on the table."

Me: "But it all goes back to LaFontaine and I don't believe him."

Several, yelling: "Why don't you believe him?"

x

Me: "Do you really think Carlos could have jumped out of a third-floor window without hurting himself?"

Aaron: "It's possible; you don't know. And maybe there was a fire escape."

Me: "But anyway, Fleming was covering the back, so how could Carlos have gotten past him?"

x

Janice, solemnly, taking off her glasses and setting them on the table: "Carlos can't remember the year he came back from Puerto Rico."

Me, feeling like Alice in Wonderland: "Do you remember the year of every trip you've made? I certainly don't. And what does that have to do with the charges against him?"

Several, shaking their heads: "He can't remember when he came back from Puerto Rico."

x

Dorothy: "I think Carlos lived in that apartment where the drugs were."

Me: "But he lived somewhere else with his girlfriend. And Hortensia Nunez said she knew all the people in the project, and she'd never seen Carlos there."

Someone: "She's a friend of Carlos's cousin. She said they were like sisters."

x

Curt: "So where do you think he gets his money? He lives in Wellesley, he wears a gold chain, he hasn't got a job."

Me: "I agree that's suspicious. Maybe he's into something. But I don't think he's been proven guilty of this. That's what we have to focus on, these specific charges."

Curt, repeating himself: "All the evidence you need is right here on the table. If you weren't so emotional, you could see it."

x

Ralph: "I don't think the pay stub is so important."

Me: "It's important if LaFontaine is lying about finding it in the apartment."

Ralph: "So you think LaFontaine is making it all up?"

Me: "I think LaFontaine made a half-assed identification, and now he has to stand by it."

Ralph: "If he made a mistake, why wouldn't he just admit it?"

Me: "Because Carlos laughed at him. Carlos got his goat."

x

Aaron: "You know, Carlos can always appeal."

x

Curt, late in the afternoon: "I know how we can end this. We could load this gun and shoot you." I *think* he was joking.

Me: "May I have a last request? Could I try the cocaine first and die happy?"

Several people laughed, the laughter of released tension. Thank goodness I could still make jokes. I was still somewhat the self I knew, a self that was being assaulted as never before. But the laughter quickly died, and the assault continued. Just as I was beginning to feel that I would never escape that hot room and those angry faces, the court officer knocked on the door and entered the room. "Are you close to reaching a verdict?" he asked.

"I'm afraid not," Aaron answered.

"Then the judge wants to speak to you. Bring your things."

As we gathered our belongings, Ralph said, "Well, I for one can't come back on Monday. My children are coming for a visit, and I have to take care of them."

I prayed that none of us would have to come back on Monday.

We filed into the courtroom and took our seats in the jury box. Carlos Montilla, sitting between his attorney and the interpreter, looked dazed and weary. For the first time, I saw the attorney speak directly to him, and Montilla nodded. LaFontaine, still sitting at the prosecutor's table, turned in his chair to face the jury box and stared directly at me, almost leering. Did he know I was the holdout?

"All rise," the clerk called out, and we stood as Judge Steele entered from his chambers and climbed the steps to the bench. He read the charge for deadlocked juries. Listening, I felt even more isolated, as if the judge too were urging me to give in. The essence was, Just get on with it and reach a verdict. No other jury will be any more intelligent or competent. Listen to each other's points of view and don't be rigid. Complete certainty is rarely possible. He concluded, "I want you all to return on Monday, refreshed and with open minds."

The long afternoon was finally over, and I walked as fast I could to my apartment on Beacon Hill, only a ten-minute walk even with a weary mind and trembling legs. In my serene and familiar home, I gave way to the tears that I had held back all day. I lay down on the bed and cried for a long time, then prayed aloud, "Please God, give me one person to stand with me. Just one."

six

AFTER THE TEARS AND THE prayer, I slept as if I had been drugged and awoke unrefreshed and headachy, two hours later. It was seven o'clock. My bedroom was stifling, and the small oscillating fan hardly made a dent in the hot, humid air. My head was thick with half-sleep and nagging questions. Was I crazy? Why was my vision so different from all the others? Had I been taken in? Was Carlos Montilla really a drug kingpin, and this was the best case they could make against him? Was I being foolish and unreasonable to hold out alone?

The ringing of the phone interrupted my thoughts. It was a friend asking if I wanted to go for a walk along the river. Yes, I certainly did. The Charles River Esplanade, beautiful in any season, was a special place, a solace for spirit and body, where I took long walks every day, almost always alone, enjoying the solitude as a kind of meditation. Now, in my bruised state, I craved the reassuring presence of a friend.

The sun was setting as Martie and I walked along the river, the red disk the only color in the gray heat-haze. Unable to keep silent about the trial — and my trial — I told her everything. She listened sympathetically, making all the right noises, and then said, "You know what's happening, don't you? You're attacking their belief systems. It's very important to them to trust the police. Otherwise, who's going to protect them from all the horrible things out there?"

Why hadn't I realized that? They wanted to believe LaFontaine, and my attempts to discredit him only hardened their resolve. Like the defense attorney, I was making them choose between an officer of the law and the dark-skinned Other who could not speak their language.

Martie was the only person I confided in that weekend. Almost all of my other friends were out of town, escaping from city heat to country heat. The bookstore was closed on Saturdays in July and August, so I had no contact with customers. I thought about calling my mother and sister in Tulsa, but did not. Wounded and mostly solitary, I gathered my forces for what lay ahead on Monday. I could hardly sleep or eat, and thought of almost nothing but the trial, even dreaming about it.

On Saturday, as I was washing the lunch dishes, looking out the kitchen window at the lovely urban view of leaves and bricks and patches of sky, I had a flash: Where are his trousers? The linchpin of the prosecution's case was that Carlos had no identification on him because he was not wearing his own clothes, having escaped clad only in his red underwear. So, where were his own trousers? Wouldn't they logically be in the apartment? But LaFontaine had admitted that nothing was found in the apartment that belonged to Carlos except the little pay stub.

Both my conscious and unconscious mind were so focused on the trial that I could not read or even watch television without returning to it. By Sunday night I was confident in my judgment that Carlos had not been proven guilty. In fact, I was almost certain that he was innocent. Maybe he had done something, but not what he was charged with.

I organized my thoughts and wrote down the major points on 4" x 6" index cards, using the mahogany dining table as a desk. With these compelling arguments, surely I could prove that Carlos was not guilty. The burden of proof, I knew from Friday's experience in the jury room, was not on the prosecution after all, but the defense. And thanks to Martie's insight, I now realized that I had to present my arguments without attacking LaFontaine. I would argue that it was a case of mistaken identity, an honest mistake on his part.

I saw myself as the Henry Fonda character in *Twelve Angry Men*, persuading the others one by one. Who would be the last holdout? Joey? Curt? I fantasized about the scene after the "not guilty" verdict was read, when the others gathered around to congratulate me for standing my ground. "It's a good thing you held out," they would say. "We were about to make a terrible mistake."

On Monday morning, after a fitful night's sleep, I was a nervous wreck, unable to eat anything except a few bites of toast. I reviewed my index cards with shaking hands and drank glass after glass of water trying to relieve my dry mouth. Many trips to the bathroom later and mouth still dry, I left my apartment, my safe nest, again wearing my only good summer dress, washed and ironed on Sunday for its third appearance in court.

Halfway up Beacon Street, near the State House, Janice caught up with me. "Did you have a good weekend?" she asked.

"Well, I did a lot of thinking," I answered.

She nodded and then made a joke. "I'm glad to see you. I thought LaFontaine might put out a contract on you."

"If he did, he missed. I'm still here." *Yes, I'm still here.*

When we arrived at the jury room, the court officer told us that we had been switched to the room down the hall, where we had had lunch on Friday. It was a cooler room, he explained, but later I wondered if the judge had suggested a change of scene in the hope of breaking Friday's pattern.

Cassie came in wearing a raspberry linen dress, bandbox fresh. Tricia was early too, and we four women made idle chit-chat, never mentioning Friday's impasse. Then Tricia told us her nightmare over the weekend: "I dreamed Carlos was chasing me through the house with a gun and threatening to kill me if I convicted him. I was really terrified. Can he find out where we live?" *This is what I'm up against,* I said to myself.

Dorothy arrived distraught. Her son had had a seizure the night before, and she had left him at the hospital to come here. She had just spoken to the judge about being excused, but he had told her if she was not present he would have to declare a mistrial. Ralph had been excused on Friday; with Ruth replacing him, we were down to twelve with no alternates left.

I felt Dorothy's silent reproach: *If you hadn't been so unreasonable, I could now be at my son's side.*

We began deliberating again shortly after ten, with instructions from the judge to start afresh with Ruth substituting for Ralph. I sat at one end of the table, Aaron at the other, like the host and hostess of a dinner party. We were silent for several minutes as Ruth scrutinized the exhibits. She then looked up and asked, "Why didn't they fingerprint the gun?"

Aaron shot me an admonishing look before explaining to Ruth that I was the lone holdout for acquittal and that I had improperly introduced information about fingerprinting. She asked to hear what I had told the others, listened, and then said,

"I need more time before I make up my mind, although I think he's probably guilty."

Could I be Henry Fonda and turn them all around? With my note cards and a glass of water in front of me, I began. "I've done a lot of thinking over the weekend, and I hope we can come to an agreement this morning. I have some strong doubts about the defendant's guilt, but maybe I'm missing something. If you can answer my questions, then we can reach a verdict. I would like for us to do that, but we need to focus on my doubts about his guilt, not your doubts of his innocence."

They seemed to be listening, grudging but quiet, and I began to go through my arguments, some already raised on Friday and some new. One by one they dismissed them. They had an answer for everything.

Three hours later, hoarse and weary, I came to the last two cards. Why hadn't I given up hope by then? There was no sign of anyone being swayed by my arguments; I had not gained an inch. But hope dies hard, and it was still breathing. I pressed on.

Curt hissed with exasperation, the sound of vented steam, as I began to speak. "This is really pissing me off," he said. "How much longer do we have to listen to you?"

Looking directly into his pale eyes, I said, "Please bear with me. I'm sorry to irritate you, but there's more I need to say." He twisted in his chair and looked at the ceiling.

I began again, leading up to the question that came to me over the weekend, a question that went to the heart of the prosecution's case. "Let's assume we accept the scenario the prosecution wants us to believe. Carlos was the man LaFontaine saw in the apartment in his red underwear. He jumped out the third-floor window without attracting Fleming's attention and without injuring himself. He ran somewhere where he found a shirt, pants, a belt, shoes, and socks that fit him. He also got a fifty-dollar bill. But he didn't stay there where it was safe. He went and stood on a street corner in plain sight and didn't run away when the police approached him." Reciting that scenario, I silently pleaded, *Can't you see how implausible it is?*

Their faces were stony and resentful, and no one met my eyes as I went on. "If we accept that version, it only makes sense that Carlos had no ID on him when he was picked up, because he wasn't wearing his own pants. So here's my question. If he wasn't wearing his own pants, where were they? Where were his trousers?"

Aaron nodded. "That's a good question."

"They must have been in the apartment," Tricia offered.

"Right," I agreed. "But they didn't find anything that belonged to Carlos except the pay stub. If his pants with his personal items were there, why aren't we looking at more solid evidence than that flimsy piece of paper?"

They sat in silence; no one seemed to have an answer. Then Curt made a stab at it. "Maybe his pants were in the kitchen, and he put them on before he went out the window."

Joey, who had been looking more sullen than usual, lit up with relief at this answer. "Yeah, Carlos was wearing his own pants."

"But then why didn't he have any identification on him?" I protested.

"Drug dealers don't carry no identification," Esther said.

I was Alice in Wonderland again; Carlos was guilty if he wasn't wearing his own pants and guilty if he was.

"How much more have you got there?" Curt asked, pointing to the index cards.

"I only have one more question to raise before I'm done," I said, "and that's about the hairdo. We heard over and over that the suspect had a Michael Jackson hairdo. LaFontaine said it several times, and it was part of the description that went out over the radio. Burch remembered it. But people can have different ideas about what Michael Jackson's hair looks like. Does anyone remember how else the suspect's hair was described?"

As usual, it was Aaron who remembered. "I think they said something about long, greasy ringlets."

I nodded. "Yes, I remember that too. So here's my problem. Fleming only saw the suspect at a distance of at least three hundred feet, without binoculars, at night. He couldn't see the suspect's face well enough to identify him, but he could see long ringlets. That must have been a fairly dramatic hairdo for him to describe it as he did."

Holding up the mug shot, I said, "But look at this. Would you describe this as a Michael Jackson hairdo with long, greasy ringlets if you saw it at night, without binoculars, from at least three hundred feet away?"

Dorothy spoke without looking at the mug shot. "He could have cut his hair before they picked him up."

I was stunned for a moment. "That doesn't seem plausible to me. Remember that he didn't have much time. Only half an hour or so went by before Burch spotted him on the corner."

Esther had another explanation. "He could have used mousse to make the ringlets, and when the mousse dried the ringlets shrunk up."

There was no polite answer to that one. Still holding the mug shot in my hand, I looked around the table. Cassie and two or three other people had said nothing. Would one of them stand with me? "Before we go any further, I need to ask a question. Does anyone share my doubts?"

Curt spoke up immediately. "I was thinking over the weekend it's not right that just one person can hold us up like this. It's absolutely ridiculous. He's guilty, and you feel sorry for him. That's all there is to this mess."

Dorothy, sitting next to him, crossed her arms as she spoke. "I have to go with our side."

"*Our* side?" I repeated the words as a question.

"I know I shouldn't say that," she said quickly, "but that's the way I feel."

One by one the others spoke.

Mildred: "I thought about it all weekend. He's guilty."

Joey: "Look at the facts. The cops all saw him."

Aaron: "I stand by my original position."

Ruth: "I don't want drugs and guns on my street." Mostly silent until now, she spoke these words with a fierceness that surprised me.

Esther: "I know a drug dealer when I see one."

Janice: "I really wanted him to be innocent, but I believe he's guilty. I think he was going back and forth."

"And you all think he's been *proven* guilty beyond a reasonable doubt?" I asked. I was so exhausted that I could taste nausea in my mouth. We must have had a lunch break, but I can't remember eating anything; lunch is a total blank in my memory.

"You've sure got some weird ideas about reasonable doubt," Joey said in disgust.

I saw an opening, one last chance. "Okay, let's hear again the judge's charge about presumed innocent and reasonable doubt." I not only wanted to be clear in my own mind but

74

hoped that as we listened to the charge again, read by the judge, someone might have a change of heart.

Aaron wrote a note to the judge and delivered it to the court officer outside. I leaned back in my chair, silent. As we waited to be called to the courtroom, Aaron raised the issue of the gun charge. In his authoritative manner, I read this message: "Now that we've dispensed with this nuisance, let's finish up." Again, he expressed his own opinion first. "I would vote not guilty on that charge. There is less evidence for it, since only LaFontaine saw the incident."

"How can you say that?" Dorothy blurted out. "That's ridiculous." I silently agreed with her. The same applied to the drug charge — only LaFontaine had identified Carlos, and all the evidence went back to him. If his testimony was enough to convict Carlos of drug trafficking, it was enough to convict him of carrying an illegal firearm. But if it wasn't enough, then Carlos was innocent on both counts.

Others joined in the noisy debate. I hardly listened, but Aaron seemed to be outnumbered. I watched them wrangle as if through a pane of glass, glad that someone else was the target, at least for now.

The court officer came to escort us to the courtroom. We sat in our usual places in the box and listened as the judge re-read part of his instructions to us. I kept my eyes away from the defendant's table and leaned forward in my chair to concentrate on what the judge was saying.

These are the words I remember best: "In order to convict you must have an absolute conviction, to a moral certainty, that the defendant has been proven guilty beyond a reasonable doubt." I repeated the words in a whisper: "an absolute conviction, to a moral certainty."

Back upstairs in the jury room, everyone ignored me, as if they had written me off. No one seemed to have been swayed by the judge's words. Looking for a place to be alone, I opened a door in the wall behind Aaron's chair and found a small coat closet. I caught Aaron's eye and said to him and anyone else who was listening, "This may sound silly, but I'm going in here for a few minutes." As I closed the door behind me, I could hear them continuing to argue about the gun charge.

Alone in the dark airless room, I groped for a light but found nothing. I knelt, wanting to pray for strength, but as soon as my knees touched the floor, I began to cry. I could not stop the tears of exhaustion and bitter disappointment, but I cried as silently as I could, my hand pressed to my mouth, so that no one would hear me. Then I forgot them, those outside the door.

I was in a world so dark I could not imagine light, in a world where only I existed, completely alone. I whispered a prayer: "Help me, help me." I don't know how long I was in that dark place before I returned, suddenly calm. I waited a moment, dried my face and eyes on the hem of my skirt, and stood up, steadying myself with a hand on the wall. I took a few deep breaths and opened the door.

The light dazzled me; how bright that room was, with its eleven squabbling strangers who ignored me as I stepped out of the closet and closed the door behind me. Was this the room I had left only a few minutes ago? Was it my eyes or the world that had changed?

I walked to the other end of the table, where my empty chair was pulled out from the others, and sat down, listening to them argue about the gun charge. At the first pause I spoke, my mouth so dry I could hardly form the words: "I have something to say."

They looked at me, and I said simply, "I'm sorry, but we have a hung jury. I cannot in good conscience vote to convict."

There were disgusted looks, long-suffering sighs, and a few curses.

"It's time to tell the judge that we are deadlocked," I said. "There's no point in going on."

"What if he tells us to come back tomorrow?" Aaron asked me.

"I'm not coming back here again," I said as firmly as I could.

Dorothy turned to Aaron, acknowledging that they were back on the same side. "So what happens now?"

Aaron winced. "They'll have to go through another trial, or they may decide not to retry him, in which case the joke's on us." *The joke?*

Janice then spoke. "It's clear she's not going to change her mind. Would any of you?"

I had not expected this, but the little bird of hope died forever as they all remained silent. They were silent too as I wrote a note on the pale-green computer paper.

I would like to see the judge in chambers. I am the dissenting juror, and after deep and painful deliberation, I cannot in good conscience change my vote. I see no purpose in further deliberations.

With a shaking hand, I signed my name.

Aaron took the note from me and delivered it to the court officer. As we waited, I sat in my chair away from the others, with my eyes closed. The others began to speak, one by one. It felt like a ritual stoning.

I heard Ruth say in exasperation, "Linda, we've spent a long time listening to you. Now you should listen to us."

"Save your breath," someone said. "She's not listening."

Then Curt's sarcastic voice: "Self-pity is not in order. You have no right to feel sorry for yourself. You're not the victim here." I opened my eyes and looked into a face as mean as any I ever hope to see. Now I both watched and listened to the others.

Dorothy, whose son was in the hospital: "I only came here today not to let you all down."

Tricia: "It's such a shame that we've wasted all this time."

Mildred, the older woman, seemed on the verge of tears: "I feel ridiculed."

Joey: "Was it Mrs. Salazar? You think it was mistaken identity?"

I nodded, even though it was not just Mrs. Salazar.

Joey, standing up: "How can you think he's completely innocent? Look at the facts!"

Janice: "She's looking at the facts as she sees them."

Joey, leaning over the table to shout at me: "Look at the facts!"

"Shut up, Joey," said the silent young woman who seemed to know him. Those are the only words I remember her saying throughout the trial. I was grateful for them.

Janice, smiling wryly: "Well, Carlos will send you roses tonight."

It was Curt's turn, a familiar tirade: "One person shouldn't be allowed to keep us from reaching a verdict. You just feel sorry for him. You're blinded by emotion and can't see the truth." He angrily tapped the juror's handbook in front of him on the table. "You're wearing a blindfold, just like she is." I was so tired that the irony of his words didn't strike me until later. He was pointing to the portrait of Justice holding her scales.

I sat listening to them, waiting for the court officer to return, close to collapse but finding strength in an inner voice that repeated, "It's almost over, and you'll never have to see any of these people again. It's almost over…"

❧

"Mr. Foreman, are you hopelessly deadlocked?" the judge asked.

"Yes, we are, Your Honor," responded Aaron, who was sitting next to me on the right. We were no longer in our usual seats.

Judge Steele read aloud for the record my note to him, pausing as he got to the word "juror," unable for a moment to read my handwriting, and then continuing. "I reluctantly declare a mistrial," he announced after he finished. He rapped his gavel, the clerk said, "All rise," and we stood for the last time as the judge departed. It was almost three o'clock. After three days of testimony and ten hours of deliberation, the trial had ended without a verdict.

I was one of the last to emerge from the jury box; several of the others were already clustered around the prosecutor, undoubtedly offering their condolences. I walked past the defendant's table with barely a glance but could see that no one there was smiling. Outside the courtroom some of the other jurors were waiting in front of the elevators. I headed for the stairs, and home.

Looking for sympathy, I stopped at the bookstore to tell Sue what had happened. She listened intently and then commented, "You know, the Chinese believe that if you save someone's life, you're responsible for him forever."

"But I didn't save his life," I protested.

"Responsible forever," she repeated.

seven

I AWOKE THE MORNING AFTER the mistrial with new energy, fueled by outrage. By telephone and in person, I told my story to family and friends, as obsessed as the Ancient Mariner.

When I called my sister, Susie, in Tulsa, she was not surprised. "You've always been a champion of the underdog," she said.

"I have? I don't remember that."

"Yes, ever since you were a little bitty girl. You would say, 'It's not fair,' and Mother would say, 'Fair is just a nice word.'"

I wondered why my younger sister remembered these things clearly and I only vaguely and upon her prompting. It always amazes me how memories can differ, *Rashomon*-like. I remember that when Susie and I were little girls, I used my fertile imagination to tease her, once even pretending to be a witch who had taken over her sister's body. Decades later when I expressed remorse for my sometimes cruel teasing as a child, Susie trumped my memory with this rosy picture: "Linda, you always took care of me. That's what I remember."

Mother had gotten the first call, as she always did — triumph or tragedy, a lawsuit won or a heart bruised, she was the first to know. All five of us children adored our mother and turned to her for comfort and wisdom. I was the oldest; after me, sixteen months apart, came Susie, then my brother Tom, and then the fraternal twins, Mike and Tim. When the twins were born, I was only four, and my mother had three babies in diapers. Somehow she made us all feel special. Talking among ourselves as adults, we discovered that we were each convinced that we were Mother's favorite. She, of course, never owned up, saying we were all her favorite.

"I'm proud of you," Mother said, after hearing the story. "Not many people would have that much courage." But she cautioned me not to get too emotionally involved in the case. "I don't want you to get hurt."

Although I don't remember always being a champion of the underdog, as Susie claimed, I know that I have a strong sense of justice and fair play. In fact, it was an outraged sense of justice that had given me the courage fourteen years earlier, in 1974, to join four other women as named plaintiffs in a class-action sex discrimination suit against the educational publishing company where we worked as textbook editors in the secondary English department.

We had always known that men had higher salaries and more "perks" than women in the company, and almost accepted it. "He's a Harvard man" was our department head's explanation when a new and inexperienced employee was given an office ("a door, a window, and a rug" was how we described that perk) instead of a cubicle. "He has a family to support" was another rationale for higher pay. We did not challenge its logic to say, "If people were paid on the basis of need, the janitor with five kids would make more than any of you." In my early years at the company, women were called by their first names, while men were addressed as "Mr. So-and-So." When a new man in the department asked us to call him by his first name, he was promptly chastised and had to retract: the other men did not want the precedent.

Over the years, the status quo became less and less acceptable to us. We grumbled when we were passed over for promotion; we chafed when our male bosses took credit for our work. We were closer to assaulting the barricades than we realized. When it happened, it was rage, not liberty that led the charge.

One autumn, five of us found out by accident, from more than one source, the salaries of the three men in our department. The two older men were making about twice as much as we were; one of them had no more responsibility than any of us. But most galling was the salary of a recently hired young man. With less experience and no more responsibility, he too made several thousand dollars a year more than any of us, a gap of almost fifty percent. I felt betrayed. In my eight years at the company, I had been praised for excellent work as an editor, and I had even been given an office. I had literally been patted on the head and told I was a good girl. Those words of praise were debased coins of little value, but how I hoarded them.

Once our rage subsided, we decided to handle the matter within the company by taking our concerns directly to management. We did not want a lawsuit. We were hoping for acknowledgement of the inequities that existed not only in our department but throughout the company, and we wanted a commitment to rectify those inequities within three years or so. That effort to keep it within the company ended when one of the upper managers threatened to fire us on a Friday. By Monday, we had found a law firm that was perfect for us, committed to social justice and willing to take our case on a contingency basis.

It was agonizing for me to defy the male authority figures. I had always had their approval and I cherished it, never having felt my own father's approval. The system was paternalistic, and I was a favorite daughter. I felt very privileged when the president of the company gave me a long, private interview. The five of us had met as a group with the other managers, but he wanted to talk with me alone. Now it seemed I was on the verge of putting myself forever beyond the pale.

With a heavy heart but certain I was doing the right thing, I joined the other four women in a formal complaint charging the company with sex discrimination. Three years later, after much struggle and uncertainty, our class-action suit was settled in a landmark consent decree, resulting in back-pay awards for more than two hundred women. The money was nice, of course — it paid for my share of the bookstore — but the most valuable rewards were psychological.

I don't know if I could have held my own in the jury room if I hadn't been through that lawsuit first. Then, of course, I was one of five, and I never could have gone the distance alone. But the challenge of standing up against strong opposition for what I believed was right had toughened me. It served as basic training for my ordeal in the jury room.

The unfairness I had seen there stunned and truly outraged me. In a round of phone calls to friends, I ranted about the other jurors: "They weren't impartial. They had one standard for the prosecution witnesses and a different, much more demanding one for the defense witnesses. They bent over backwards to believe the prosecution and not once did they give the defendant the benefit of the doubt, not once. They didn't treat Carlos the way they'd want to be treated. They just weren't fair."

A friend interjected a cautionary note that brought me up short: "You don't want to get too self-righteous about it." After we hung up, I smarted for a while, and then realized she was right. I had to watch it.

I was driven by outrage but also by a sense that I was caught up in something larger than myself. A chain of coincidences had led me to that jury box: Carlos's trial began on the day I had chosen at random, I was in his jury pool, I was not challenged. It did not seem to be merely an accident. I believed that there was a purpose in my being on that jury, not just for Carlos but also for me.

That summer I was one of the forty million viewers mesmerized by Joseph Campbell's talks with Bill Moyers on the PBS series *The Power of Myth*. His central thesis was that the same myths recur in every culture and reflect universal psychological experiences. The story of Jonah and the whale, for example, is a standard motif, Campbell told us. It represents a descent into the darkness from which you return transformed; the belly of the whale is a symbol of the power that is stored in the unconscious.

After the trial, I thought about the Jonah story and my experience in the jury-room closet. Was I in the belly of the whale? I pondered this for a while and then scolded myself, Oh, come off it — you spent five minutes in a closet. But something did happen to me in that dark room, something profound that changed me. I am still trying to understand it. Perhaps I had for the first time come in touch with my deepest instincts and trusted them as never before. Certainly I had never been so alone, or my trust in myself so tested.

On the Friday night after the mistrial, I watched the next program in the series, "Sacrifice and Bliss." Campbell told a true story that I will never forget, that gave me goose bumps as I listened to it.

In Hawaii a few years before, two police officers were driving along a cliff road, past a windy spot where many suicides had jumped to their deaths. Seeing a young man there, poised to leap, they stopped the car, and the officer on the right ran to the young man, grabbing him just as he jumped. It was almost too late. The officer was himself being pulled over and would have plunged to his own death, but his partner had arrived in the nick of time and saved both men from going over the precipice.

"Why didn't you let go?" a reporter asked the first officer later. "You could have been killed." Why had everything in that man's life dropped away at that moment — his duty to his family, to himself, to his job, all his wishes and hopes for life?

"I couldn't let go," he answered. "If I had let go of that young man I could not have lived another day of my life."

Campbell was illustrating a question raised by Schopenhauer. How is it that one can so participate in the peril and pain of another, that without thought, spontaneously, one sacrifices one's own life? Campbell told us Schopenhauer's compelling answer to his own question. *In a moment of psychological crisis, this metaphysical truth breaks through: you and the other are one, you are the same being, bonded together as one. And the realization of that bond is the truth of your life, what makes you fully alive.*

The day after the mistrial I called Jim Hamilton, one of our attorneys in the class-action suit and a former president of the

Civil Liberties Union of Massachusetts, to tell him what had happened.

"I can't believe what a coincidence this is," Jim said. His former wife, to whom he had not spoken for some time, had called him the day before, deeply upset. She had just finished serving as a juror in the trial of a black man accused of drug dealing. She thought he had not been proven guilty, but no one else agreed. "The other jurors jumped all over her, she finally gave in, and now she feels terrible. That's why she called me," Jim explained. It was extraordinary to hear a story so similar to mine, and I hated to think of my guilt and remorse if I had given in.

"Jim, I need your advice," I went on. "I want to contact the defense attorney, but I don't know if it's proper or even legal. What do you think?"

Jim thought that there was no problem, but wanted to double-check with a friend who was the current president of the Massachusetts civil liberties union. He called me back two days later with a green light. "Harvey knows of nothing to prevent you from contacting Blair. Attorneys aren't supposed to contact jurors, but there seems to be no reason you can't get in touch with him." And Harvey had told Jim, "If she gets in trouble, I want to represent her." Jim said he had replied, "No, I want to represent her." Finally, Jim told me, they agreed that if I got in trouble they would do it together.

With the reassurance of two ace attorneys at my side if I ended up in the dock, I plunged ahead and called Blair. I left a message with his secretary and told her I was the holdout on the Montilla case.

"We are very grateful to you," she said. We talked for a while, and then I asked her name, which I had missed.

"I'm Evelin," she said.

"Oh, the same name as Carlos's girlfriend," I replied.

I could hear the amusement in her voice as she answered, "The same person. That's me." I was glad to hear it. With more than a professional connection to the case, Blair might be glad to hear my perspective as a juror.

I wanted to contact Blair for two compelling reasons: to see if I could be of help in the retrial and to find out if my instincts had been right about Carlos and LaFontaine. When I held out in the jury room, I was not sure that Carlos was innocent, only that he had not been treated fairly.

"You were right," Blair told me when we finally spoke after a lengthy game of telephone tag. "Carlos is innocent. And I'll tell you this. I've represented a fair number of criminals in my time, and they've all lied to me at least once. But Carlos has never lied to me."

Blair also confirmed my instincts about LaFontaine — he was a notorious bad apple. "I have a friend who's high up in the police department, and he tells me they've been trying to get LaFontaine off the force for years, but the union keeps standing up for him. He's been disciplined dozens of times, but all that is confidential. I tried to get access to his record, so I could bring it up at trial, but the judge denied my motion. At the retrial, I'm going to say from the beginning that LaFontaine is lying."

"I'm not sure that's a good idea," I cautioned. "I've learned that people don't want to believe that a cop is lying. And if you make them choose between Carlos and an officer of the law, it's no contest. One woman actually said, 'I have to go with *our* side.'"

"So that's what I'm up against," Blair sighed. "I didn't realize there was so much prejudice."

"I'm afraid so," I answered. "Will you let me help you next time? I learned a lot in that jury room, and I know what bothered people. I could be the spy who's just returned from behind enemy lines."

Blair laughed and said he'd be delighted to have my assistance. We made an appointment to meet for lunch.

Three days after the mistrial I wrote a letter to Judge Steele, identifying myself as the dissenting juror in the Montilla trial.

"...After serving on this jury, I have grave doubts that a Spanish-speaking defendant can get a fair trial when police officers testify against him. Because of an overwhelming bias in favor of the officers' testimony, the defendant was never given the benefit of the doubt.... I plan to discuss this apparent injustice with a friend who was formerly president of the Civil Liberties Union of Massachusetts and perhaps write an article about my experiences on this jury. Please confirm for me that I am free to discuss the jury's deliberations and the details of the case now that the trial is over...."

The letter was answered promptly, not by the judge but by the court's information officer. After expressing regret that my jury deliberations were "so unsettling," the writer assured me that I was at liberty to discuss the case and my experience as a juror.

Warren Blair and I met for lunch at the Parker House lounge on a Friday, eleven days after the mistrial. He was there before me, sitting at the bar drinking a glass of champagne. He ordered a glass for me, and we settled ourselves at a marble-topped table in the corner of the lounge, furnished with brown-leather club chairs and velour loveseats.

"Why didn't the prosecutor challenge me?" I asked Blair right away. "What was she looking for when she excused people?"

"She was trying to get rid of anyone who might be too liberal," he answered.

"But the class-action suit was right there on my question-naire. Wouldn't that give her a clue that I was on the liberal side?"

"She was probably focusing on the bookstore. Small business owners are known to be law-and-order types," Blair said.

I had to laugh. "Not at this small business."

Another question was much on my mind. "How can Carlos and Evelin afford to live in Wellesley? That really bothered people, and I wondered about it, too."

"Oh, they live in a project, subsidized housing," he answered. "I understand it's quite nice."

"I had no idea there was subsidized housing in Wellesley. You must make sure the jury knows that next time, or they'll imagine him living in a mansion bought with his drug profits."

Blair shook his head. "And the truth is, they don't have two nickels to rub together." He then told me how he had gotten involved in the case. Carlos and Evelin had originally hired someone else. They borrowed $3,000 from relatives to pay him a retainer. The attorney urged Carlos to plead guilty to a reduced charge. Carlos refused. "I'm not going to plead guilty. It wasn't me." On the eve of Carlos's first scheduled trial, almost a year before, Evelin came to Blair in tears and begged him to help. "I couldn't say no," Blair explained, "even though I don't usually do this sort of case. Most of my work is malpractice and personal injury."

"Are you going to call Rudy Muchuca as a witness again?" I asked. "He was very damaging, you know. I thought he must either be confused or lying."

Blair grimaced as he answered. "Rudy won't be on the stand again. He got all confused. They didn't eat together that day. And Carlos doesn't know Pablo Osario; he's never even seen him. The Pablo that Rudy was talking about is Carlos's cousin."

"It must be difficult to prepare witnesses who don't speak English," I offered.

"Tell me about it," Blair said. "I couldn't even talk to Carlos unless Evelin was there to translate."

"A client you can't talk to and a police officer who's lying. Sounds like you had two strikes against you from the beginning."

"Yes, and believe it or not, LaFontaine has always had good luck with juries. Until that mistrial you caused, he'd gotten automatic convictions, or so I'm told." Blair repeated the street talk he'd heard about LaFontaine. "He's terrorizing the Hispanic community. He steals their money and drugs and pistol-whips them, men *and* women. And they can't do anything about it."

"But isn't he Spanish himself?"

"That's right. He's from Puerto Rico."

"Why does he pick on his own people?"

Blair shrugged. "Who knows what drives a person like that to do what he does? My father was a police commander, and I've always had great respect for cops. I hate it when someone like LaFontaine makes the good cops look bad too." Fleming was the one who testified at the grand jury hearing, Blair said, because LaFontaine was suspended at the time for filing a false report.

"Isn't there any way you can get at his record? It's just not fair that the jury thinks he's a good, honest cop."

"I could try to subpoena his file, but the judge will probably turn me down. All that internal affairs stuff is confidential."

At the end of lunch, over coffee, I found out what had happened in the courthouse plaza that Thursday during the trial, when LaFontaine was talking to Carlos and Evelin at lunch and afterwards Carlos was not in court. LaFontaine had said to Carlos, "Things are not going well for you. You're going to prison. You'd better run away now before it's too late." Carlos was so terrified that he became ill and had to go to the hospital for a tranquilizer. Blair went on, "I didn't know where the hell he was."

"It sounds to me like LaFontaine is on a power trip," I said.

Blair was quiet for a moment. "Perhaps I shouldn't tell you this, but when the trial began, I said to LaFontaine, 'You must know it wasn't Carlos; can't you do anything for him?' And LaFontaine said, 'Tell Carlos all he's going to get from me is a jar of grease.'"

A jar of grease? Then it registered: for the rapes in prison.

At that moment, LaFontaine the real man — tawdry, corrupt, and destined to be broken — vanished into a symbol of evil, malevolent and heartless. When Blair and I parted after our two-hour lunch, I was even more resolved to do everything I could to help Carlos. Surely the truth would win out if we fought hard enough.

eight

"CARLOS IS A DIFFERENT PERSON because of this," Evelin told me over the phone, sometime in August. "He was such a baby, and I kept telling him, 'You've got to take some responsibility. I'm not your mother.' But he's very hardheaded and won't listen. He never took the arrest seriously. 'They can't do anything to me,' he said. 'It wasn't me.' But when the trial started he got scared. Now he's afraid of what he might lose, and he's changed."

A skilled legal secretary and bilingual, Evelin could earn more than Carlos. She worked full-time, while he, when he could find a job, worked part-time in the mornings, to have afternoons free to take care of their baby, Carlos Jr., and Josua, Evelin's seven-year-old son by another man. "Carlos is the only father Josua has ever known," Blair had told me, "and he calls him 'Daddy.'"

Carlos was twenty-four years old, born in the Dominican Republic but a U.S. resident alien since he was sixteen, living first in Puerto Rico and then coming to Boston, where he had lived for four years. Evelin, a year older, was born in Boston of Puerto Rican parents and grew up here. She had always dated professional men, until Carlos swept her off her feet three years before.

"He was kind of a playboy back then," Evelin also told me. (How much of a playboy I did not learn until later.) "But he began to change when the baby was born, and now with all that's happened, he's not the same person."

"Why don't you get married?" I asked.

"Carlos wants to, but I don't know. I'm still not sure."

I thought that Carlos would look better to a jury if he were married, but I was in no position to urge marriage on anyone else, having remained single myself. (No one ever made me an offer I couldn't refuse.) Now that I was nearing fifty, there were few eligible men of a suitable age, and even fewer who were attractive to me as well. Those rarities, almost always, wanted a younger woman. But several months before the trial, I had met an interesting older man, a tall, silver-haired bank executive. "David" had possibilities.

"He's a great catch," a friend advised me. "Play your cards right and snag him." But playing games to catch someone was against my nature, and I probably wouldn't have succeeded even if I'd tried. Recently divorced, David was quite skittish and kept a certain distance. Nevertheless, the prospect of romance with an attractive, eligible man intrigued me, and I enjoyed our occasional times together.

One night in September, as David prepared dinner for the two of us in the kitchen of his Beacon Hill duplex, I sat on a stool, watching him cook, and talked about Carlos's case.

"I don't get it," he said. "You were just one of his jurors. Why are you going to so much trouble for him?"

"Because I saw the bias in the jury room, and I don't think he can get a fair trial without my help."

"You think you're some kind of wonder woman?" he asked, smiling.

I laughed. "Definitely not, but it's funny you said that. A few nights ago I dreamed that someone ran to tell the prosecutor, 'She's threatening to fly.' Sure enough, the very next night I was flying over the treetops, invisible."

"Sounds to me like you've gone off the deep end," he said, slipping sole fillets into a pan sizzling with butter. "You'd better watch it or men in white coats will cart you off in a straitjacket."

I said nothing, staring at the fish as it hissed and turned opaque.

David was not the only one who questioned my mental state, although others were not so blunt. Certainly I was obsessed, and my friends and family worried about me.

"You were dangerous back then," my friend Anne told me later. "Dangerous in a beautiful kind of way, but dangerous."

"What do you mean 'dangerous'? I asked her.

"You were a woman possessed, with a wild eye."

One night, unable to sleep, I got up at two in the morning and paced the floor in my nightgown, talking out loud to an imaginary jury. I was Carlos's lawyer, making my opening statement:

"I beg of you to keep an open mind as you search for the truth here. Carlos Montilla does not speak your language, but he is a human being just like you. Listen to the testimony as carefully as you would want the jury to listen if you were on trial. Treat him exactly the way you would want to be treated. He is not a stereotype. He is a very real person, and he's been accused of something he did not do."

Back and forth between my four-poster bed and the lowboy, I replayed the scene over and over, pleading with the jury.

Back in bed, exhausted but still unable to sleep, I listened to my heart thump for what seemed like hours. My mind raced in circles until finally, mid-loop, I fell asleep.

Although I knew it was not possible, I longed to defend Carlos myself. Blair would listen patiently and graciously to my suggestions, but I could tell his heart was not in it. He was distracted by more lucrative cases and annoyed that Carlos and Evelin had not yet been able to pay him. The court reporter would not release the trial transcript she had prepared at his request until she was paid the $850 cost, and she was badgering him for payment. Judge Steele had denied Blair's motion for the state to pay the cost, and now he was left responsible. "I'm not going to cough that up myself," Blair fumed. "I'm already in the hole on this case." We were at a great disadvantage without the transcript. The prosecutor had ordered an expedited copy immediately after the mistrial, but lacking a written record, I had to rely on my memory of what had happened.

From my experience in the jury room, I knew that images were as important as facts, if not more so — both the image of Carlos in the courtroom and the images created in jurors' minds by the testimony. "Tell Carlos to leave that silk suit in the closet," I advised Evelin. "If he looks like the stereotype of a flashy Hispanic, the jury will form a picture that's set in stone. It'll be easier to see him as a drug dealer."

"But that suit is the best clothes he has. What should he wear?"

"What about a blue blazer, khaki pants, and a white shirt? But no tie; that would be going too far, I think. He can wear the same pants and shirt he wore at the first trial. He just needs a blue jacket." Evelin promised to pass on this advice to Carlos.

As for her, I suggested that she try to look less gorgeous and well-dressed and not carry the designer handbag.

In front of the jury, I thought Blair should stress the image of Carlos standing calmly on the corner as the police approached him. That to me was not the action of a man who had just fled the scene of a crime leaving behind a gun with his fingerprints on it. "That's a good point," Blair said. "Certainly if he had run away, the prosecution would have brought that up as evidence of guilt. So it should work the other way too."

Blair was scheduled to appear in court on September 20 in front of a new judge, and I urged him to try again on a motion for the Commonwealth to pay for the transcript. If that failed, I was prepared to pay the cost myself.

"I had a fantastic day in court," a jubilant Blair announced over the phone on the afternoon of the 20th. The new judge, Elizabeth Porada, had immediately agreed to Blair's motion for the cost of the transcript; he promised me a copy as soon as he received it.

He was also filing a motion to obtain LaFontaine's internal affairs record, based on information from his contact in the police department. According to that officer, LaFontaine had been disciplined for filing false reports, receiving stolen goods, assault and battery, and other misconduct. He had twice been demoted from detective to patrolman.

Blair was adamant about my not appearing in court with him. "I don't want you there," he said flatly. Although I never pressed him for an explanation, I suspected that he was concerned about the propriety of my assisting him and also about the possible danger of LaFontaine learning who I was. Uneasy on both scores myself, I stayed away from the courthouse even though I longed to be there.

Since I was juggling two roles then, crusader for justice and bookseller, it would have been difficult anyway for me to keep showing up in court. Sue was away from Labor Day through Columbus Day on her annual holiday to Nantucket, and I was managing on my own, with the help of Melanie, the young Yale graduate who worked for us part-time, as we needed her.

Melanie, who was young enough to be my daughter, clucked over me. "You're getting too thin," she fretted. "You should try to eat more."

I had indeed lost several pounds on what I called "the stubborn juror's diet." Anxiety had robbed my appetite. "But I don't feel like eating anything but soup," I protested to Melanie. "What about mashed potatoes?" she countered. I agreed that mashed potatoes sounded good and promised to eat some.

Bookselling duties kept me busy. It was the season when books flooded into the store but only trickled out; Christmas stock arrived before customers were geared up for gift buying. Melanie unpacked the boxes of new arrivals, and I taxed my ingenuity to find places to put them. I did all of the store's bookkeeping except the yearly tax forms, and I had gotten behind in the paperwork. While Melanie was on duty at the front desk by the cash register, I worked away at the back desk, trying to catch up. Often I had a phone to my ear, doing bookstore business, talking about the Carlos case, or making plans with friends. Busy as I was, at times I found myself staring out the street-level picture window at the yellowing leaves of our linden tree, grown tall in its pit in the brick sidewalk.

Promptly at six, I closed the store and headed to the Esplanade for a long walk, a ritual that renewed me both mentally and physically. During that five-mile round trip at sunset, some of my best ideas were born. It was also the only regular training I was doing for the Nepal trek in October.

Most evenings I worked on my notes for Blair, but sometimes I was too tired to do anything except watch television, slumped in the rocking chair. One night in late September I saw a deodorant commercial set in a jury room. "He's dry, but does he smell good?" a male voiceover asked about the frazzled-looking man who was rolling up his shirtsleeves. He was the hold-out juror. "We can't reach a verdict as long as we have doubts," he said (reasonably, I thought). Others shouted at him. Then a change of scene: The others are now congratulating the hold-out, who has managed to turn them all around while still smelling good. "You were right," they say, "thank you," clapping him on the shoulder.

I laughed out loud at this replica of my own fantasy. And a fantasy it is, I learned when I read Seymour Wishman's well-known book *Anatomy of a Jury:* "No case like that of the lone dissenter who turns the jury around in *Twelve Angry Men* ever cropped up in a study of over two thousand juries." The Chicago Jury Project, cited in the book, found that ninety-five percent of verdicts reflect the majority on the first ballot; for a minority to prevail, it must be substantial — three or more jurors. "In more than nine out of ten cases, by the time jurors go into the jury room to deliberate, they have made up their minds." Only about five percent of all juries are deadlocked and do not reach a verdict. It is rarely a single stubborn juror who hangs a jury. "In the trials studied by the Jury Project, not a single jury hung with a minority of less than three."

I did not learn these facts until almost three years after my own experience. When I charged full tilt at the windmill, I had no idea all the statistics were against me, either to turn the jury around or to hold out alone. That evening, as I watched the television commercial and laughed at my old Henry Fonda fantasy, I was nursing a new one, confident that the truth would prevail, and we would win an acquittal for Carlos, or at least another hung jury.

By coincidence Blair had a new client, "Gomez," also accused by LaFontaine of drug dealing, in a similar scenario. LaFontaine claimed to have seen Gomez flush drugs down the toilet in an apartment where drug deals were allegedly going on. "The only thing is, you can't see the bathroom from where LaFontaine was standing," Blair told me. Unlike Carlos, however, Gomez spoke excellent English and knew how to stand up for himself. Both Gomez and Carlos were in court with Blair in late September, and LaFontaine was there to testify against them, strutting around in his cowboy boots. Blair described this scene in a courthouse hallway:

"Everybody hates you!" Gomez yelled. "Why are you terrorizing your own people?"

"I've been screwed too many times by Spanish people," LaFontaine shouted back. "I've been stabbed and I've been shot."

"How can you be an officer of the law when you break the law?" Gomez persisted. "You have no right to wear a badge."

Terrified by the yelling match, Carlos moved to a bench on the other side of the corridor. LaFontaine swaggered over to him, at first smooth and almost friendly. "Hey, you're a lucky guy," he said to Carlos in Spanish. "You have some woman helping you, working with your lawyer." Carlos looked at him blankly, not knowing what LaFontaine was talking about. He had not yet met me and was only dimly aware of my assistance to Blair.

"But it's not going to do you any good," LaFontaine went on. "We've got Pablo Osario in handcuffs down in the Charles Street Jail. We've made a deal with him, and he's going to say it was you there that night with him." LaFontaine smiled and walked away.

Evelin was in a state the next day. "I'm scared," she said. "What are they trying to do to us, making deals with Pablo?"

"I think LaFontaine is trying to get Carlos to run away, just like he did at the first trial," I suggested.

As we talked, Evelin calmed down a little. "Maybe it will work the other way and help us," she said. "We can probably prove he's lying, because he doesn't know anything about Carlos, and they can't coach him on personal stuff like my son's name. I have to be careful not to say it."

Evelin was typing a motion for exculpatory evidence, asking that the prosecution reveal any inducements offered to Pablo Osario and any evidence provided by him that would assist Carlos. I was not worried about Pablo as a witness. Like Evelin, I was sure he would be caught in a lie and that could work against the prosecution and be a boon for us.

Blair finally received the transcript and sent me a copy by messenger. I spent the weekend and every evening after that poring over it, looking for specific quotations to back up our case and to confront prosecution witnesses with if they tried to change their stories.

The most thrilling discovery in the transcript was LaFontaine's statement that he found Carlos's pay stub *after* Carlos was brought to the police station. (I had missed this during testimony, or it didn't register.) "After we brought him in and he gave us the name, we were still making inventory. We hadn't come across these cards we picked up. It wasn't until after that I observed in the bag the name 'Carlos Montilla,' the pay stub."

LaFontaine slipped when he made that statement, and we could use that slip against him. Blair must convince the jury that the pay stub could easily have gotten mixed up with the other papers on the table.

Of course, I didn't really think that the pay stub had been accidentally mixed up with the papers being inventoried. What I believed — and still do — is that LaFontaine knowingly and maliciously fudged the evidence about the pay stub and the underwear. He was on a power trip of arrests and convictions and wanted to make a weak case stronger. Maybe he really thought it was Carlos he had seen; maybe he deliberately framed an innocent man. Perhaps Carlos gave him a motive when he laughed at LaFontaine. "Laugh all you want," the officer had said. "I'm going to send you to prison for three years." Or perhaps LaFontaine had another motive.

nine

ALTHOUGH I HAD TALKED MANY times to Evelin on the phone, I still had not met her or Carlos in person. Somehow a meeting had never worked out, even though I thought it was essential. At the end of September, after a late lunch with Blair, I suggested that I go back to his office with him, to be there at five o'clock when Carlos came with the children to pick up Evelin.

"I want to see the baby," I told Blair. "And I need to ask Carlos a few questions and give him some coaching about his appearance on the stand."

Blair called Evelin so she could alert Carlos. "She wants to see the baby," he said, as I stood beside him at the Parker House pay phone. Then we hopped into a taxi that took us down to the waterfront, to the red-brick building on the end of Long Wharf where Blair had his Boston office.

As Blair and I walked in, Evelin stood up from the typing chair in her small work area and greeted me with a radiant smile. She seemed much softer than she had in the courtroom, and her creamy skin and doe eyes were even more striking up close. She was wearing a loose dress, a maternity dress; she was several months pregnant. The baby was due in January, she said.

Nine-month-old Carlos would have his first birthday the same month.

Blair vanished into his office and closed the door. I sat down in a chair next to Evelin, and we chatted as she continued to work, tearing apart long sheets of printed labels. Carlos was due to arrive shortly with the children, as he did every day to pick up Evelin. This day he would come upstairs, where he would meet me for the first time.

It was more than two months since that day in the courtroom when I had looked into Carlos's eyes and seen innocence. I had gone to bat for him, and his cause had filled my hours, but until now he only existed in the abstract. How would I react to him in person? Would I be disappointed? Would I lose faith or gain even more? The meeting had all the anxiety of a blind date, but worse.

I saw the little boy first, seven-year-old Josua, with a beautiful face like his mother's. Behind him walked Carlos, carrying the baby. We smiled shyly at each other. He looked smaller and younger than I remembered, and even more childlike. The baby in his arms was a miniature, moustache-less copy of himself: the same luminous eyes with thick curly lashes, the same full, pouty lips. Even the wispy, black curls that clung to the baby's scalp were an embryonic version of his father's hair.

Carlos sat down next to us and spoke in Spanish to Evelin, who said to me, "He wants to thank you for what you did for him. He is very grateful." More words in Spanish, as Carlos looked from the baby to me. Evelin translated, "He says, 'I'm so afraid they're going to take me away from my son.'"

We carried on our conversation with Evelin translating. Carlos jiggled his son on his knees so the baby was doing a little dance; they were thoroughly happy with each other.

"Does he remember me from the jury?" I asked.

"Oh, yes," Evelin answered. "He told me, 'That woman keeps staring at me. I think she wants me to go to jail.' He doesn't remember anyone else, just you. No one else looked at him."

"I know they looked at him; in fact, one of the women commented on how good-looking he was. But they didn't really see him. They saw a picture they already had in their heads. That's why what he wears is so important," I said, bringing up a subject that I considered crucial.

"We got a blue jacket like you suggested," Evelin explained. "When he looked in the mirror, he said, 'It's not me.'"

Unable to conceal a smile, I said, "Tell him if he wants to look pretty when he goes to prison, that's up to him."

"That's exactly what I told him," Evelin said, laughing.

"I have some questions to go over with him and some ideas about his testimony. When does he want to do that?"

"*Ahora*," Carlos answered, a word I remembered from high-school Spanish. "Now."

As good a time as any. "First of all, I don't think you should refer to Evelin as your girlfriend. Just call her Evelin, or better yet, call her your wife. If Beland challenges you, you could always say that in your heart, she's your wife."

Carlos shook his head. "Evelin," he said emphatically. This was my first direct sign of his almost stubborn truthfulness.

Evelin took the baby in her lap as I coached Carlos on how to present himself on the stand. "Sit up straight, keep your head up." He dutifully straightened, but his knees began to jiggle just as they had in the courtroom, obviously a nervous habit. I put an admonishing hand on his leg. "Don't jiggle your knees. Try to keep still."

More admonitions: "Don't say LaFontaine is making up stories about you, because people don't want to believe a cop is lying. Don't volunteer anything, like going back to Puerto Rico. Just answer the questions." I knew this was a lot for him to absorb, but he seemed to understand, nodding after Evelin translated my words. "And why did you keep saying you weren't working for money?"

Carlos answered, "I was helping my friend, but he was paying me off the books. I didn't want to get him into trouble."

"I wouldn't worry about that. They're not going to do anything to your friend. Just say you were working part-time at the restaurant, or the jury will wonder where you got money for taxis and the fifty-dollar bill you had on you."

I asked about the information on the arrest booking sheet. Carlos said that LaFontaine filled it out, and he told the officer his social security number, which he knew by heart. He had lost the card some time before. He was pretty sure he had his keys with him the night of the incident, but he couldn't be certain.

"Did they take only your money and jewelry from you?" I asked. "Only what was listed in the box on the booking sheet?"

"No, they took everything. Even my shoelaces."

"Okay, so only things of value were listed on the booking sheet." (Beland must have known that; she had gotten in a low blow with her question about the keys.) "Make sure that's clear. The items in the box were just your money and jewelry, not everything that was taken from you. And don't insist you had two chains and ninety dollars."

I was curious about the photo that LaFontaine had waved in front of Carlos at the station, saying it was a picture of Carlos. Could he remember anything about it? No, he could not see it at all. LaFontaine had only flashed it by him.

"What did you think when LaFontaine told you to take down your pants?" I asked.

"I didn't know what to think," Carlos answered. "I was shocked."

Blair had come out of his office in time to hear this last exchange. "Why are you bringing that up?" he asked me.

"So the jurors will know why Carlos hesitated to take down his pants. Otherwise they'll think he was trying to hide the red underwear he was wearing that LaFontaine would recognize."

Blair nodded. "Okay, I see."

A few more questions revealed that Carlos had never been in a police station before that incident and didn't know what to expect. "Good, good," I told him. "Be sure to say that."

Then Carlos added, "LaFontaine told me that he was taking the underwear to test it for gunpowder."

Blair gave me a look. "That's the first I've heard about that. I should ask for the results of those tests."

The baby was fussing, and Evelin handed him to Josua, who had been quietly listening from a seat on the floor. "You're being a very good boy," I said to Josua, as he stood up to take his baby brother. He acknowledged my praise with a gratified smile and gave his mother a sidelong glance. I had a feeling he was not always quite this good.

I had more to go over with Carlos, and they needed to leave; Carlos's cousin Anna was expecting them for dinner. There were two questions I had to ask first.

"Carlos, I am certain that you were not the man LaFontaine saw that night. But did you ever sell drugs?" As Evelin translated my question, her large eyes probed Carlos's face. She seemed as curious about his answer as I was.

"No," he said firmly, without looking at us, his eyes straight ahead.

"Do you use drugs?" I asked.

Again he answered "No," shaking his head. Then, after a moment's pause in which he seemed to be thinking, he added, "Beer. I drink beer."

I felt that he was telling the truth. I knew that I wanted to believe him and might be deluding myself, but my instincts told me I was hearing the truth.

Carlos and Evelin prepared to leave, but I stayed behind, to talk more to Blair. We said our goodbyes near the door, Carlos holding his son in his arms. Unable to resist the baby's soft, caramel cheek, I gave him a little kiss, which seemed to startle him. His eyes and mouth rounded, and he swiveled his head to look up at his father, who smiled reassuringly at him. Then, as if I had gotten an okay, little Carlos turned back to me with a smile that turned his face from solemn to impish.

Carlos shook my hand and said, "Thank you for all your help. I hope someday God will pay you back." I felt a bond between us now, an inexplicable connection.

Blair and I continued our conversation over a drink at the bar next door, a noisy, smoke-filled yuppie hangout. I learned to my dismay that he had not yet read the transcript. "I'm up to my ears in other things," he explained. "But I'll get to it this weekend for sure." He was in a better mood about the case. Not only had the judge come through for the cost of the transcript, but Carlos and Evelin had managed, by borrowing again, to pay him part of his fee.

The latest word on Pablo Osario was that the prosecution was not calling him after all. "Maybe they realized that there was no way they could coach him to be convincing in his lies about Carlos," I suggested.

"I was thinking of calling him myself," Blair said, "maybe asking for them to be tried together, but it's too late. Pablo's back on the street."

"How could that happen? He's wanted for this case."

"Who knows?" Blair shrugged. "He probably paid a small bail and got out."

"Pablo must have told them something they didn't want to hear," I said. "They wanted him out of the picture. Isn't there any way you could find him? I think he could really help us."

"If Pablo has any sense, he's long gone by now," Blair replied. "I'm sure that's a lost cause."

Another postponement of the trial gave me a second chance to meet with Carlos and Evelin. For that final session, two days before my departure for Nepal, we sat huddled together in Evelin's work area, with Carlos in the typing chair. I began by confirming an important point. "Was that pay stub the only thing you had with your name on it?"

Yes, it was; that's why he always carried it with him. He had lost everything else. I remembered Carlos's testimony that LaFontaine had gone through his papers, one by one. He must have been disappointed to find only one flimsy pay stub with Carlos's name on it, but that had been enough for eleven jurors. This time Blair must be sure that the jury knew that Carlos had nothing else with his name on it and always carried the pay stub with him. Wouldn't they find it implausible that he had dropped it like a calling card at the scene?

Evelin then told me of an exchange she had with LaFontaine the week before, when they were all in court for the scheduled retrial that was postponed. "How can you be so sure it was Carlos?" she had asked him. LaFontaine replied, "Well, I might be mistaken." She had pounced on that. "You might have made a mistake?" LaFontaine smiled and said, "But then again, I might not have." What kind of cat-and-mouse game was he playing?

The defense witnesses had been notified to appear on the following Tuesday, when Blair estimated he would begin presenting his case. Evelin was preparing a subpoena for that day for the fingerprinting expert from the police department, who would give an authoritative statement of facts to discredit LaFontaine if he repeated the same testimony he had given at the first trial.

There was some good news on the witness front. Carlos had remembered another man from the club that night, the friend who had gone to the jail to post bail for him. "He was right there under our noses all the time," Evelin said.

"And the Salazars will be there for sure?" I asked.

"Oh, yes, they want to help Carlos. They know he is innocent." Evelin then told me that Salazar had had his own run-in with LaFontaine. "It didn't have anything to do with Carlos. LaFontaine and his partner came into the club looking for drugs. When they didn't find anything, LaFontaine beat up Salazar."

"Did Salazar press charges?" I asked.

"No, he was too afraid. LaFontaine told him, 'I could arrest you for spitting on the floor.'"

I didn't like the sound of this. "Are you sure Salazar will show up again for Carlos? He must be afraid of retaliation."

"Oh, yes, he wants to be there. And we'll go by to pick them up," Evelin reassured me.

I rehearsed Carlos again for his appearance on the stand, sitting him down in a chair with wooden arms. Instantly he slumped into his natural posture. "No, no, sit up straight," I said. He snapped to attention.

"Good, good. And be sure to keep your knees still. Now, pretend I'm Lynn Beland." Carlos made a face. "Look straight at me, not at the floor. And just answer the questions, nothing more. Make her drag it out of you." I made a gesture of pulling something toward me with both hands.

Blair emerged from his office and nodded his approval. I said to Carlos, "Excellent, just right," words he understood without Evelin's translation.

We were done. There was no time for more. As Carlos and Evelin left to go home, Blair had some parting advice: "Be sure to make love all you can in the next few days. It may be your last chance. If he's convicted, they take him straight from the courtroom."

I was more optimistic: "When I get back from my trip, we can go out to celebrate and drink champagne." Again, Carlos seemed to understand what I was saying, and we exchanged smiles.

In the bar next door, Blair and I found a quiet but dark spot for our last conference. I repeated Evelin's story about LaFontaine saying he might have been mistaken.

"He said that to her?" Blair was incredulous. "If I have her repeat that on the stand, it will be a bombshell."

Still, Blair was not as confident as I wanted him to be. "I think I have a one-in-five chance," he said, "but that's better than before."

"Don't even think you're going to lose," I encouraged him. "Pretend you're Paul Newman playing the part of an idealistic lawyer who's determined that evil will not triumph over good."

He brightened at the analogy. "You know, when I was fifty pounds lighter, people used to tell me I looked like Paul Newman."

The next afternoon, October 13, Blair called to report that the trial would definitely begin the next day, the day of my departure for Nepal. The other news was that Carlos had finally gotten his sartorial act together, complete with blue blazer. "He looked great, like he was going down to the yacht club," Blair said.

Sue had returned from vacation after Columbus Day not looking at all well. She had a deep cough, and her lips were blue. I was quite concerned and urged her to see a doctor, but she resisted. Fortunately, Melanie was on board to share the bookstore duties while I was away.

On Friday afternoon, after some last-minute shopping, I took a taxi to the airport with plenty of time to spare. Catching a plane always makes me nervous, and I was more than an hour early for the shuttle to Kennedy, where I would get an evening flight to Amsterdam and rendezvous the next day with Andy and the trekkers coming with him from Britain. From there it was on to Nepal via New Delhi. My long-awaited adventure was about to begin, but my mind was on what I was leaving behind.

When I returned to Boston a little over three weeks later, Sue was in the hospital, having nearly died from a rare lung infection, and Carlos was in prison.

ten

EVELIN'S VOICE ON THE PHONE was that of a woman trying to make the best of things. "Carlos asked me to call you, to thank you for all you did for him and to make sure you knew what had happened."

Yes, I knew what had happened. I had known it on my return when there was no message from Blair waiting for me, but my heart had resisted the inevitable. Perhaps the message had gone astray, or perhaps he wanted to tell me the good news in person.

My head was still partly in the Himalayas, my mind filled with indelible scenes of beauty: terraced hills like contoured green velvet and bright-yellow fields of mustard; the Himalayan peaks in the moonlight, gleaming ethereal and white under a star-filled sky; misty forests of giant rhododendron trees, their gnarled trunks draped with Spanish moss, their bark the color of frosted burgundy — such a forest is said to have inspired Tolkien's *Lord of the Rings*. And too, the radiant, welcoming smiles of the Nepalese villagers and the camaraderie with my fellow trekkers and the crew, especially when we sang and danced together around the campfire at night, to the music of a mouth organ.

The memory of the physical challenges was already beginning to fade. The steep ups and downs of the narrow, zigzagging trails were so demanding that I sometimes staggered into the campsite at the end of the day and collapsed in my tent until dinner. Sleeping on hard ground and bathing from a basin were minor in comparison. Some parts of the trail took all my resources to navigate: narrow makeshift paths through scree landslides that could be set off again at any moment; swaying, rickety, single-plank suspension bridges far above rushing rivers; and most daunting, a slab ledge curving around a jagged rock face, with nothing on the other side except open space — and a long, long fall to the rocks below. I had survived all those obstacles, not knowing that an even more difficult trek lay ahead.

When I still had not heard anything four days after my return, I called Blair's office, hoping against hope. Neither Blair nor Evelin was there, but the woman who answered the phone told me what I dreaded to hear. Carlos had been found guilty and sentenced to three to five years in prison. They had taken him straight from the courtroom just as Blair had warned.

I imagined the scene. LaFontaine and Beland exchange smug, victorious smiles. Carlos, wearing handcuffs and the blue blazer that is not him, looks back at Evelin with frightened eyes as the bailiff leads him from the courtroom.

What went wrong? Evelin, when she called a few days later, told me some of it. Things went much faster this time. The trial was finished early on Monday afternoon, and none of the defense witnesses were in court, having been told they would probably testify on Tuesday. Carlos and Evelin had gone by the

Salazars on Monday morning to pick them up, just in case, but they were not home. A neighbor said they were out of town.

Evelin didn't know why Blair had not asked for a continuance. "And he didn't put Carlos on the stand. Carlos feels cheated he never had a chance to tell his story." He was now at Concord State Prison, awaiting assignment. Could I write a letter to the social worker on his behalf? He had heard that the Spanish men were being sent to Bridgewater and that it was a terrible place. I promised to write a letter immediately; it was in the mail the next day.

"I thought I had won; that's why I didn't put Carlos on the stand," Blair explained when I called him a week or so later. "After what happened the first time, I didn't want to risk it." What it boiled down to, Blair said, was credibility. The jury believed LaFontaine even though Blair caught him in several lies and elicited testimony that he had been twice demoted to patrolman.

The case went to the jury about one o'clock on Monday. At 4:30 they were still deliberating, and the judge sent them a message to return the next day, after sleeping on it. The foreman replied that they didn't want to come back and would reach a verdict. At 5:15 the jury returned, and much to Blair's astonishment, Carlos was found guilty on both charges. The judge, who may have drawn a different conclusion from the testimony, wanted to bypass the mandatory sentence of three to five years, but the prosecutor intervened, insisting on the full term. "The judge really had no choice; it's the law," Blair said.

While the transcript of that trial later became available to me, I knew that if I read it, I would feel like a helpless ghost in the courtroom. *No, no, put him on the stand. He'll do all right, I know he will. Ask for a continuance so the jury can hear his witnesses.* There I'd be, in a nightmare of paralysis, feeling the agony but unable to intervene.

On a visit to Sue in the hospital, I told her the story of Carlos's second jury not wanting to come back the next day. She responded with these words, delivered in her dry style: "And wretches hang that jurymen may dine."

"What's that from?" I asked, not recognizing the quotation.

"Alexander Pope, *Rape of the Lock*, Smith English class" was her answer.

I was astounded at both the aptness of the line and the quickness with which it sprang from Sue's memory to her lips, almost like a reflex. (In more mundane matters, such as the names of bookstore customers, Sue's memory was not always so facile.) After a check with *Bartlett's*, I copied the couplet in red ink on the cover of the manila folder that became my Carlos file. The words served as a motto for what happened to Carlos, and who knows how many others before and after Pope penned them in 1712.

The hungry judges soon the sentence sign,
And wretches hang that jurymen may dine.

Did one or two or more holdouts crumble under pressure to reach a verdict? Did someone on the second jury have important plans for the next day? Was it all part of an inexorable fate for Carlos, a fate that now also had me in its grasp?

Talking to Evelin felt like the final curtain. What else could I do for Carlos, other than writing the letter to his social worker? In a symbolic act of closure, I threw away my copy of the transcript from the first trial, stored in the bottom drawer of the small oak desk in my bedroom. I held the thick stack of papers in my hands for a few seconds before dropping it in the wastebasket.

Thump, and it was gone: the Commonwealth of Massachusetts versus Carlos Montilla, more than three-hundred typewritten pages, many of them marked in red with my notes and underlining. All that effort, all that futile effort.

I turned to walk out of the room but had taken only a few steps before something inside me said, *NO!* I retrieved the transcript, feeling as if I had made a rescue in the nick of time. I did not understand what held me back, but I could not perform that symbolic act and let go.

The transcript sat undisturbed back in the desk drawer for several weeks, a period of deep depression for me. I sold books, visited Sue in the hospital, made phone calls to get patrons and sponsors for the Beacon Hill Civic Association Winter Dance coming up at the end of January, showed friends my slides from Nepal, smiled and laughed and joked, but a black cloud covered the sun.

A bitter pill stuck in my throat that I could neither swallow nor spit out. I could not bear the fact that an innocent man was in prison, his life perhaps ruined, while a corrupt cop continued on his power trip of arbitrary arrests and wrongful convictions. Was there no way to reverse such a blatant injustice? I told the story again and again, in outrage and in the hope of reaching someone who could help. Hardly anyone who came into the bookstore escaped, not even Richie the parcel postman. Fortunately, I had a visual aid to snag my listeners.

The *Boston Globe* had accepted my short article about my jury experience and printed it while I was in Nepal. Writing the story, back in August, had been a struggle. I went through draft after draft, about twenty-five in all, and consulted a dozen friends. These collaborators, these friendly twelve, gave me a much-needed sense of support after my loneliness in the jury room.

The story was printed on the second page of Focus, the editorial section of the Sunday *Globe*. Complete with illustration — a drawing of a lone woman in a jury box — the story took up most of the bottom half of the page. The headline read "The Jury System on Trial," with a subtitle, "Juror finds 'classic mob scene: townspeople hounding the outsider.'"

To photocopy the story I had to go to a shop with an extra-large machine and then trim the pages. A stack of twenty or so photocopies, replenished again and again, sat on a shelf in the bookstore, ready to be dispensed whenever I detected a sympathetic or even politely interested ear.

As November went on, I grew more and more depressed. The bare trees, with only a few bronze-colored oak leaves still hanging on, were like a mirror of my spirit. Still, I was more grateful than ever for my own fortunate life, and my daily prayer of gratitude became even more fervent. I prayed too for strength and guidance. These prayers were a gleam of light in my melancholy.

My mood was darkened even more by a chance encounter one Sunday afternoon as I was walking down Newbury Street. Two women approached from the other direction, carrying parcels and talking animatedly to each other. The shorter one on the right with streaked blonde hair looked familiar. Where had I seen her before? She was casually dressed and out of context, but after a moment or two I recognized the big eyes and the broad, hunched shoulders: Beland. She glanced at me with no sign of recognition, laughing with her friend.

She's won. She and LaFontaine have won. Those heavy words of defeat resounded in my head as I looked away from her and walked on. *They have won.*

The last Monday in November, a dark, rainy day, my spirits were at their lowest ebb. I had lunch that day in Newton with my friend Jane from high school, and she immediately sensed my mood when she picked me up at the trolley stop. Jane and I had been good friends at Central High School in Tulsa, and I was delighted when she, too, had settled in the Boston area after a stint in California. Our friendship had grown even deeper over the years.

We ate at an upscale cafeteria with lots of oak and hanging plants and a healthy menu. Next to the cash register were copies of *The Wall Street Journal,* a paper I admired but rarely read. A front-page headline jumped out at me: "Trial and Error: Cases in Which a Juror Recants Leave Law Without Remedy. Policy Is to Let Verdicts Stand Lest Panels Be Hounded, But Result Is Troubling." I bought a copy and set it on my tray but tried to resist reading it over lunch.

I could see the concern in Jane's brown eyes as she gently drew me out to talk — a psychotherapist by trade, she was an intuitive listener. She knew the whole story, of course, but she hadn't realized how downhearted I had become. "I feel so helpless," I told her. "I don't know what to do." There was nothing Jane could say except the kind, comforting words of a good friend.

Alone in the trolley car back to Boston, with rain pelting the windows, I read the *Wall Street Journal* story, written by two staff reporters. Its message could be summed up in one disheartening sentence: A jury's verdict is as good as set in stone.

Even when there are serious problems with a jury, it is almost impossible to overturn its verdict.

"Judges have repeatedly ruled that verdicts can't be overturned on the basis of a juror's change of heart," the article read. "Their reasoning is simple and powerful. If jury decisions could be easily reversed, jurors could forever be hounded — or threatened — by dissatisfied defendants." It is an inherent risk of the system, but there is no way for jurors to change votes they renounce or to correct mistakes. In one case cited, the jurors had decided that the defendant had acted in self-defense when he killed a man and wounded another. They checked "involuntary manslaughter" on the verdict sheet, thinking that meant justifiable homicide and non-guilt. To their horror, the defendant was sent to prison despite their testimony that they had made a procedural mistake. "The court ruled that the manslaughter verdict, however unintended, would stand."

One holdout on a murder trial relented in the end only under pressure from other jurors. Her subsequent efforts, along with another juror, to get the verdict overturned had come to naught. Despite some new evidence that might have created reasonable doubt, the judge refused a new trial, because doing so, he said in court, "would undermine our whole jury system."

The article also raised the issue of hasty verdicts, especially in long trials when jurors grow impatient to return to their normal routines. It cited a case I had read about in July, of Ventura Morales, a Mexican migrant worker convicted of murder in Oregon. One of the recanting jurors, part of a support group for Morales (ultimately successful in winning his freedom), admitted she had a reasonable doubt about his guilt when she voted to convict him. But after a three-week trial, she and others were anxious to get back to their lives. "Some, she says, didn't want to miss the start of duck-hunting season." *And wretches hang....*

The *Journal* story plunged me deeper into gloom. Even if all twelve jurors on Carlos's second trial recanted, the verdict would stand. The jury had spoken, and that was that. I remembered Aaron's cavalier remark as he tried to persuade me to change my vote: "Carlos can always appeal."

That night, in complete despair, I cried myself to sleep, my eyes stinging with bitter tears. When I awoke the next morning, sunshine was dancing through the lace curtains. My inner sun was back too, wan and wintry but out from behind the dark cloud. That rebound of the spirit, experienced before in my life, always seems a miracle. Along with the sun, hope returned too, pale but determined. There must be a way to set right this injustice. I had to keep trying.

One evening early in December, as David the banker and I were walking through the Public Garden on the way to a Newbury Street restaurant, I told him about my renewed determination to help Carlos.

"Haven't you considered that he might be guilty?" David asked. "After all, twenty-three out of twenty-four people thought so. Were they all wrong?" He spoke in a clipped, businesslike manner, as if he were addressing a board meeting instead of a dinner date.

"Yes," I said. "They're wrong. And if I weren't sure he was innocent, I wouldn't be so disturbed by the injustice of it."

"Well, I think it's time for you to back off and let things take their natural course."

"But they're not taking their natural course. I can't back off, I just can't. I feel that I have no choice. I have to do all I can to help him. I don't think it was an accident I was on his jury —"

He laughed. "Let's leave the supernatural out of this."

"There's another reason I can't let go," I said, acknowledging what I had just admitted to myself. "I want to be proven right. I want to win."

David turned to me and smiled. "Now *that* I can understand."

❧

I had not talked to Evelin since the phone conversation that seemed to be the final curtain. Now that my spirits were restored, I wanted to get in touch to let her know I was still interested and to find out how Carlos was doing. Around the middle of December, I called her one evening at home.

As Carlos had feared, he was sent to Bridgewater, a name I knew only as a state prison for mentally disturbed inmates. What was he doing *there*? It must be a dreadful mistake. He would be classified on January 4, and the social worker said if his outstanding traffic tickets were not cleared up by then, he could not be transferred to a minimum-security prison. He would have to serve his time at Bridgewater. Worst of all, they had told Carlos he would be deported after serving his sentence, devastating news for him. "He knows I won't go with him," Evelin said. "He will lose everything."

She began to sob. "He's threatening to kill himself. I don't know what to do. I don't know what's going to happen."

eleven

ENTER THE THREE WHITE KNIGHTS, in order of their appearance in the story.

First White Knight: Ed DeMore, a neighbor and friend, who lived with his wife, Paula, and four children quite near my bookstore. Half Italian, half Irish, Ed was of medium height, with an athletic build and a self-confident gait, rolling his shoulders a bit as he walked. He had an open and friendly face but projected a sense that he was not a man to be crossed. Three years earlier, Ed had quit his job as a high-powered financial executive to take a long-thought-about sabbatical. During that year off, before he started his own small company, Ed often came into the store to order books; he was reading voraciously, mostly psychology and sociology, and attending divinity school classes. He now sported a close-cropped beard, and with his lower face covered, the twinkle in his blue eyes and the laugh lines around them were more apparent.

I had seen Ed in action when we worked together on the board of the neighborhood association. Very persuasive and articulate, he not only proposed ideas but followed through on them. He got things done. During that gloomy November when I was telling Carlos's story over and over in the hopes of reaching the right ear, I thought about Ed. I knew if he became involved, something would happen.

Sometime after Thanksgiving, Ed finally came into the bookstore. After chatting a while, I gave him a copy of my jury article, which he had missed when it appeared in the *Globe*. He sat down in the wooden chair in front of the desk and listened as I told him the rest of the story: how Carlos had been convicted by the second jury, how he'd never been in trouble with the law before, how he had been primary caregiver for his baby son, and what I had learned about LaFontaine.

"Do you have a transcript from your trial?" Ed asked. A flash of memory: the transcript in my wastebasket. Thank God I had retrieved it and could answer yes. "I'll ask a lawyer friend to look at it," Ed said. "Let me talk to him and get back to you."

Ed took my jury article home and talked it over with his wife. He had already been thinking he would like to do something to help others directly, not just writing checks for charity fundraisers. "This could be one of those things," he told Paula. With her approval, he decided to get involved.

When I learned from Evelin the alarming news about Carlos, I had not yet heard back from Ed. I was in a state of near-panic, desperate for immediate legal help for Carlos. It didn't seem possible that his future could hinge on unpaid traffic tickets. The morning after my conversation with Evelin, I once again called my lawyer friend Jim Hamilton, promptly at nine. After explaining the situation, I told him I wanted legal help.

"Let me be sure I understand," Jim said. "You want to retain an attorney?"

"Yes, I want to retain an attorney," I answered boldly. Jim said he would talk to his partner and get back to me. I had no idea how much an attorney would cost or how I would pay for it. Jim and his colleagues had taken our sex-discrimination case on a contingency basis, so I was insulated from the reality of legal costs. But I had a small nest egg and a good amount of equity in my apartment. I would cross that bridge later.

Later that morning, I called Ed to find out if he had talked to his lawyer friend. Yes, he had spoken to Mike Keating, who lived around the corner from him and whom I knew only slightly. Mike immediately agreed to look at the transcript. "I don't know if you realize this," he told Ed, "but I'm very interested in the whole issue of justice." The next step, Ed said, was a meeting with Mike, and he would arrange it.

It was Jim Hamilton who came up with an emergency stopgap. "I've got someone for you," he said when he called me back that afternoon. Anne Braudy, with the Massachusetts Correctional Legal Services, would meet with me right away, as a favor to Jim and at no charge. Jim had also gotten the scoop on the Bridgewater situation. There were three facilities there, not just the mental hospital; the other two were a maximum-security prison, Old Colony, and a medium-security prison, Southeastern Correctional, which was supposed to be not too bad. Jim thought that Carlos was most likely at Southeastern, and that turned out to be the case.

Anne Braudy met with me the next afternoon at the European-style café where I had coffee almost every morning. We sat in the corner by the window, with a view of passersby on Charles Street. A small, brown-haired woman with a diffident manner, Anne seemed an unlikely advocate for prisoners' rights.

I had expected someone more brash. She spoke in a soft voice while I jotted down notes on a white pad.

She could help Carlos with the traffic tickets, and if necessary, they could be cleared up after classification, which could then be appealed. The threat of deportation was a bigger problem. Although Carlos was a legal alien, his felony conviction meant almost certain deportation after serving his sentence. "Jim told me you were prepared to make a financial commitment," Anne said. "What Carlos is really going to need is a good immigration lawyer, as soon as he's ready for parole."

"I understand that will be in the next few months," I said. "That's what they told him at Concord."

Anne shook her head. "I don't think so. With a mandatory sentence of three years, he won't be eligible for parole for two years." *Two years!* She had other discouraging news. If the INS put a detainer on Carlos, which was almost certain, it would be hard for him to be transferred to a minimum-security prison because he would be considered a flight risk. Anne also suggested that if Carlos and Evelin were planning to marry, they should do it as soon as possible. "While he's in prison?" I asked. "Yes, they can do that," she said.

Carlos and Evelin spoke on the phone every day. She could not call him, but he could phone her collect at certain times. When she told him that I had called, he was astonished that I was still interested. "Carlos is so happy," Evelin reported. "He says, 'Now I can sleep. I know she's special, and she can help me.'"

"Don't let him get his hopes too high," I cautioned. "I don't know if I can do anything or not."

Carlos no longer threatened to kill himself, but his moments of hope alternated with black moods. "Don't come see me," he told Evelin. "Don't send me food or money. I don't want to be dependent on you. I don't want to be a burden on anyone." Evelin would have none of it. "Carlos, give me a break. I'm not going to abandon you. You're the father of my children. You haven't always been the best of the best, but lately you've been the best. And if I don't support you, who's going to?"

"Carlos is very fortunate to have you," I told her. "Not many women would be so loyal."

"What he's most afraid of is that the baby will forget him," she said. "At first when we visited, the baby jumped all over him, but then less and less, and Carlos could see the baby pulling away. But then yesterday the baby jumped all over him again, and he was so happy." I remembered my first meeting with Carlos in Blair's office: the baby in his arms, the happy love between them, and Carlos's words, "I'm so afraid they're going to take me away from my son." I had never had a child myself, to my regret, but I knew that if Evelin stopped going to see Carlos regularly, the bond between him and his son would be broken and his worst fears would come true.

I knew Mike Keating by sight as a neighbor and by reputation as a top-notch corporate attorney who occasionally appeared on the local news. A renowned litigator, Mike later became even more famous with the publication of the 1995 bestseller *A Civil Action;* he was one of the lawyers who had defended W.R. Grace in a notorious pollution case.

Mike had Irish good looks, with thick, sandy hair and a face that was both boyish and strong. A sense of great integrity was immediate and compelling. He was slightly built, with small hands and feet, and always seemed to be in a hurry. When I saw him on the street, he was usually charging along, arms pumping, briefcase in hand. Other times I saw him driving a blue station wagon loaded with children. Although Mike and his wife, Marty, whom I knew better, lived with their two sons and young daughter quite nearby, he rarely came into the bookstore. I never would have approached him on my own. Ed was the vital link.

On December 21st, Ed and I met with Mike at his law firm, Foley, Hoag, & Eliot. The elegant reception area, with an enormous Oriental rug and plush beige couches, had a corner view of the financial district through tall picture windows. We waited there until Mike, in his lawyer-uniform of pinstripes and white shirt, came to escort us to a small conference room.

We talked for a while about juries, a subject of great interest to Mike. "I do a lot of work with mock juries," he said. "It's always fascinating." A neighbor who knew Mike well had given him my *Globe* article in October, saying, "You must read this." The story had intrigued him, but he had been too busy to talk to me about it as he had intended.

I told Mike what I knew about the second trial, and he said, "If I were in Blair's place, I probably would have waived the jury after what happened the first time." Why hadn't Blair thought of that? I wondered, especially since Judge Elizabeth Porada seemed to be fair, and not just a prosecutor in black robes, as I had heard some judges were. In Massachusetts jury trials, the judge is forbidden to comment on the evidence. In a bench trial, the verdict is up to the judge, and from what I now knew, a bench trial would be my choice if I were innocent. If I were guilty, I'd take my chances with a jury.

Mike would read the transcript sometime over the holidays and then give it to a colleague in his office, a former prosecutor named Gary Crossen, who had just joined the firm.

Crossen had been an assistant district attorney for five years in the Suffolk County D.A.'s office (the same office that had prosecuted Carlos) and then served for five years as an assistant U.S. attorney, heading up the Criminal Justice division. He would have joined us that day, but he was out of town.

Then I asked Mike the big question. "What is the best way to get Carlos out of prison?"

"Probably by getting the goods on LaFontaine," Mike answered. Hire a private investigator and find proof that LaFontaine lied, maybe even suppressed evidence that would have cleared Carlos. Then we could go to the D.A.'s office with what we knew and ask for a new trial, with a designated disposition. "It's been a long time since I have been involved in anything like this," Mike told us. As a young lawyer, he worked for several years as an advocate for prisoners' rights. Now a partner in the prestigious firm of Foley, Hoag, he handled mostly corporate cases.

Nothing dramatic happened at that first meeting. Although sympathetic and interested, Mike was careful not to commit himself to anything more than reading the transcript. But there was no question in my mind that he was the perfect person to help Carlos and that he would. I didn't even consider looking elsewhere; my search was over.

The Second White Knight, whether he knew it or not, was on the road.

Carlos and Gabriel, an inmate who spoke a little English, sat on the cot in Carlos's cell, using the bureau, pulled close to the bed, as a desk. Carlos wrote out on a white lined pad what he wanted to say, and Gabriel helped him translate. Spanish to English to Spanish to English, for over an hour. When they were done, Carlos took out the Happy New Year card Evelin had found for him to send. There was a poinsettia on the cover and a printed message inside: "A warm note of thanks/To say people like you/Help make the world brighter/By the nice things you do!" On the blank left-hand side he laboriously printed his own words. I received it the next day and read it with tears in my eyes.

> I dedicate this card to the best person in this world. The person more distinguished and sensitive, inteligent. The person who rush to help me in a darkness of my life. I dedicate to you Linda Cox with all my affection because I never will think see a person like you in this country. That in a moment like this enlarge my filling and make diferent my soul happy. Before I don't belived that I will find some-body who gift me he hand in this bitter moment and I found you.
>
> You came to relieve my ache and I appreciate that. Thank you for everything that you doing for me. You are deserve the all merit that anybody can gived in this life.
>
> Thank you for everything again and God bless you from Carlos Montilla, who wish the best to you.

The card arrived the day I was leaving for Tulsa to spend Christmas with my family. Before catching the plane I quickly wrote a card back to Carlos, telling him I would do everything I could to help him. "Many good people know about you and want to help too. I know God will show us the way. Please do not lose hope. I pray that prison will not take away your sweetness...."

After my return, I showed Carlos's card to Ed. "You must have been very touched," he said. "Maybe because of what he's going through, he'll end up changed for the better. He might have kept on waffling in his life if this hadn't happened."

"Yes, I think that's true," I replied, "as long as his life isn't ruined."

"We won't let that happen," Ed said emphatically. No response could have cheered me more.

It also cheered me when Ed called a week or so later to say that a meeting had been scheduled to meet with Gary Crossen, the young former prosecutor, and Mike. The first hurdle, Ed said, was Gary's reaction when he learned that I was the lone holdout for acquittal of the twenty-four jurors who heard Carlos's case. "Twenty-three to one!" Gary had scoffed. "The guy must be guilty. Remember, I'm a prosecutor." But he had agreed to read the transcript as a favor to Mike, who had helped bring him into the firm.

❦

Gary Crossen looked much too young and unjaded to have a ten-year record as a prosecutor. Tall and thin, with wavy brown hair, he had the small features and pale, freckled skin of a boy. Without his moustache and wire-rimmed glasses, he probably could have passed for a teenager, although he was actually thirty-seven. In repose, his face was impassive, revealing little except through the eyes, which were remarkably direct and intelligent.

We all sat, that January morning, in the same small conference room where Mike had met with Ed and me before Christmas. After some initial chit-chat, I showed Mike and Gary a photograph of Carlos and his family. This was Ed's idea: "Get a photo, if you can; these are family men." Evelin had promptly provided me with one that was taken in their home when Carlos Jr. was a few months old. It was a classic triangle composition, with Evelin at the peak, sitting on a chair above the others. Carlos, kneeling beside her and foreshortened, could have been her child. He smiled at the camera shyly, his fingertips resting on the handle of the baby carrier where Carlos Jr. appeared to be asleep. A somber-faced Josua sat on the floor in front of Carlos, his arm embracing the baby carrier.

Gary studied the photograph for a few seconds and passed it to Mike without comment.

"He doesn't look like a junkie, does he?" Ed offered.

Mike replied, "No, he doesn't."

Without further ado, Gary got down to business. "When Mike asked me to review the transcript I thought I'd be one hundred percent convinced that the guy belonged in jail," Gary began.

"After all," I interjected, "it was twenty-three to one."

Gary gave me a slightly surprised look, not knowing that I had heard about his reaction through Ed. "But I wasn't," he continued. He was disturbed by Fleming's testimony, his refusal to be pinned down on any particular aspect of the suspect's appearance — "partners usually back each other up as much as possible" — and that Fleming was no longer LaFontaine's partner. Unless something untoward happened, officers almost always remained partners.

"And the arrest seemed odd to me," Gary said. He thought there must be some information that had been withheld; perhaps an informer, perhaps even Pablo himself, had made a deal with the cops. "The suspect's description could fit almost any Hispanic male. They must have had Carlos's name, maybe from someone with a grudge."

"I thought it was just bad luck, that he stepped outside for a breath of air at the wrong time," I commented.

Gary shook his head. "No, that seems too pat to me." He went on to say that in his reading of the transcript, there was enough evidence to convict, depending on which testimony you believed.

"I didn't think the prosecution provided the burden of proof," Mike said. "The evidence was very thin."

"That's the defense attorney's point of view," Gary smiled.

Mike looked at me and said, "I probably would have done what you did."

"But withstood the pressure less gracefully," Gary teased. (I was getting my first sign of the congenial rivalry between Mike and Gary and of Gary's playful side.)

Laughing, Mike again addressed me. "I commend you for sticking to your beliefs, but the others stuck to theirs too."

"Yes, they believed LaFontaine and I didn't. I really had a gut feeling about him."

Mike nodded. "Those instincts should be listened to."

"At the trial, I felt that Carlos was innocent. Now I'm sure of it. I would stake my life that Carlos was not the man LaFontaine saw that night."

"Did you ask him?" Gary inquired.

"Yes, I did."

From the look on Gary's face, I could tell that he had not expected me to say yes. "Some people don't bother to ask that critical question," he said.

Gary was aware of LaFontaine's "troubled history." Although he himself had never dealt with LaFontaine, he knew other prosecutors who had been leery of the officer and given him a wide berth. "But his history might not be as checkered as you think," Gary said.

I repeated what I had heard from Blair: the street talk that LaFontaine was terrorizing the Hispanic community, stealing their money and drugs and pistol-whipping them, men and women; the filing of false reports; the accusations of assault and battery. "Warren told me that the brass have been trying to get LaFontaine off the force for years, but the union stands up for him."

Gary responded that he knew the top people in the police department. "They've had lots of tussles with the union," he said. "If they wanted LaFontaine off the force, they could get rid of him. Officers have been fired for less." He also gave me another view of Lynn Beland, whom he knew from his days in the Suffolk County D.A.'s office: "She's accomplished, sharp, and straight. If she tried Carlos twice, she must have believed he was guilty."

I was more than happy to revise my image of Beland as LaFontaine's knowing accomplice. "Then maybe she will help us if we show her that LaFontaine was lying," I suggested.

"That's not her job," Gary replied. Still, I had hopes that if Beland was indeed a straight shooter, she would not want to protect a tainted conviction.

The next step for us, Mike said, was to hire a private investigator to find the missing pieces: information about the apartment and its occupants and about LaFontaine's history. It was a waste of time to try to prove again that Carlos was somewhere else. We had to concentrate on proving that LaFontaine was a perjurer and that exculpatory evidence was withheld.

"How much will a private investigator cost?" Ed asked.

The person that Gary had in mind charged $40 an hour, and we were probably looking at $1,000, $1,500, or maybe as much as $2,000, he said.

"And what about the lawyers?" Ed asked.

Mike answered that question. "If you can give me some maneuverability, we can continue pro bono." After the investigator's report, if there was enough to pursue the case, Mike would have to check with his partners, but he was almost certain they'd want to continue.

"No one wants to see an innocent man in prison," Gary said matter-of-factly.

After Ed and I left, I later learned, Gary turned to Mike and said, "Where on earth did you find that woman? Her head's in the clouds. She thinks she can save the world by getting a drug dealer out of jail." Despite his reservations, he was willing to take the next step, as a favor to Mike and because of what he had heard about LaFontaine.

The cast was now complete. The former prosecutor, a skeptic to the core, became the unlikely but essential Third White Knight for the defense.

The very next day, at 8:10 in the evening, I got a phone call from Mike. "Have you been listening to the news?" he asked.

"No, what's happening?"

"Two Boston police officers have been suspended for shaking down drug dealers. Guess who one of them is?"

"Albert LaFontaine!"

"Yes, I could hardly believe my ears," Mike said. "It's a big break for us. It doesn't mean we're home free, but it's a real leg up."

"I knew it had to happen sooner or later," I said, "but what a stroke of luck that it happened just now."

The moment we hung up, I did a victory dance through the apartment. I was a laughing dervish, whirling from room to room, exultant with new hope.

Both the *Boston Globe* and the *Herald* ran stories the next day about the suspension of Albert LaFontaine, 45, a sixteen-year veteran, and his rookie partner, Jose Pomales, 28. The police department's own Anti-Corruption Unit had filed the complaints against the two officers, accusing them of extorting nearly $4,000 from three occupants of an alleged drug den in Dorchester. LaFontaine was also accused of indecent assault and battery on two women in the apartment, over a span of three hours beginning about midnight January 18.

LaFontaine and Pomales arrested one man in the apartment but allegedly let the others go free in exchange for the money. The report filed by Pomales (again, LaFontaine left the report writing to his partner) said that they had followed Joseph Taylor into the Columbia Road apartment about midnight to make a drug "buy" and arrested Taylor when he tried to pull a revolver on them. Pomales also said Taylor had been selling drugs outside another Columbia Road apartment nearby. Taylor remained charged with cocaine trafficking and illegal carrying of a firearm, a police spokesman said. (I was struck by the familiar elements of this scenario.)

The *Globe* story had background on LaFontaine: According to a police commander, LaFontaine had been fired by the department a few years ago after he was found to be running a pawn shop on Centre Street in Jamaica Plain without knowledge of his superiors. The Civil Service Commission had ordered LaFontaine reinstated, but he had been demoted from detective to patrolman.

On February 1, anti-corruption investigators presented the evidence against the two officers at a closed-door magistrate's hearing in Dorchester District Court. After seventeen witnesses testified for more than four hours, the magistrate upheld the charges against both officers.

A week later Carlos and Evelin were married. I was honored and touched to be a member of the small wedding party.

twelve

"I HAVE TO TAKE OFF all my jewelry?" I repeated to Evelin as we stood in front of a locker in the prison anteroom.

"Yes, you can't wear anything inside except a wedding ring," she confirmed. "Or a religious medal."

I possessed neither of those, and off came the choker of pink crystal beads, the pink enamel earrings, the opal ring, the gold ring, the pseudo-gold Swiss watch. Without the jewelry, I felt like a nun in my white linen blouse, navy wool skirt, blue stockings, and navy shoes. Even my overcoat was navy. Evelin had said she was going to wear a plain suit, and following the etiquette my mother taught me, I dressed so as not to compete with the bride.

At the last minute, she had changed her mind and bought a white taffeta, princess-style cocktail dress with a bolero jacket. With her dark, shoulder-length hair, creamy skin, and doe eyes, she looked like a Latina beauty queen. "I wanted to do it for him," she explained. "I hope they don't say it's too low cut," she fretted, tugging at the bodice. There was a strict dress code for female visitors, designed so as not to arouse the inmates.

"But it's your wedding," I said. "Doesn't that make any difference?"

"Nothing makes any difference. They don't care. Remember, they strip-searched me when I was eight-and-a-half months pregnant."

The prison anteroom looked like a tiny bus station: lockers, a vending machine, restrooms, a double row of plastic chairs bolted together back to back. But instead of a ticket seller at the glass window, there was a prison guard who took our visitors' forms and checked our picture IDs. Waiting with us were Evelin's father, Octavio, a dark-haired attractive man in his fifties; Carlos's mother, Mirta, who had flown in from Puerto Rico for the wedding; and Divina, Evelin's friend who would perform the ceremony. We had all arrived in one car, driven by Evelin.

"Divina?" I had repeated when Evelin introduced us in the car.

"Yes, Divina," she said.

"That's a good name for a justice of the peace," I said, and she laughed. She was thirty or so and very pretty, with a mane of honey-blonde hair. "This is my first prison wedding," she had told me. "I get asked all the time because I speak Spanish, but they've never been marriages I could sanction."

She gave me an inquiring look as I stuffed a wad of tissues into my skirt pocket. "I have to be prepared," I explained. "I always cry at weddings."

The guards took us through the security check in pairs. First, Evelin and Divina, and then Mirta and me. She spoke very little English, but we exchanged sympathetic glances as the guard instructed us to remove our coats and empty our pockets. Under her coat Mirta wore a bright red dress that matched her spike-heeled shoes. She was much taller than Carlos — he had inherited his mother's face but not her height. She was two years younger than me. Carlos could easily have been my son.

At the guard's order, I stepped out of my shoes. The guard felt inside them — looking for contraband, I presume. I walked through the metal detector, and then a female guard took me into a cubicle and closed the door. She was wearing a trousered uniform, a hat, and small gold earrings, the only clue to her gender. "Have you ever done this before?" she asked in a deep voice. I shook my head. What was going to happen to me? Would I be strip-searched?

"You have a right to refuse the pat-down," she explained, "but you can't go inside if you do. Okay?"

"Okay," I said, lifting my arms cooperatively. She then patted me down, front and back, more discreetly than I expected.

When I stepped outside the cubicle, Mirta was waiting for me with her coat on. Since it was so cold, we were allowed to keep our coats with us, but as I slipped mine on, the guard pointed to the white wool scarf draped around the collar.

"Is that attached?" he asked.

No, it wasn't, and I would have to put it in the locker with our other belongings. Having rid myself of that potential instrument of murder or suicide, I was let through, and Mirta and I joined Evelin and Divina on the other side of the glass-windowed door. We stood shivering in the small vestibule, while Octavio went through the security check by himself.

The couple who were to be witnesses had taken the wrong exit and arrived at the prison half an hour after us. Now they were having a spat at the guard's window in the anteroom. After a few minutes, the guard passed the word to us in the vestibule. "They're not coming in."

Evelin slumped against the wall for a moment and then turned to me. "You'll have to be a witness."

"I'd be honored," I said.

Divina then told me, apologetically, that the ceremony would be entirely in Spanish. "Evelin asked me to do that, and I didn't know about you."

"Don't worry about it," I reassured her. "I'm sure I'll understand enough to know what's going on."

There were two guards in the vestibule with us. "You're here for a wedding?" one of them asked. He was short, with a pleasant, round face.

"Yes," I answered, "aren't you bringing the champagne?"

He laughed and said, "You won't get any champagne in here." When Evelin told him she was marrying Carlos Montilla, he nodded. "He's a nice kid."

Octavio joined us, and the other guard — the tall, silent one — led us outdoors into the prison yard. An icy wind whipped through that open space, and I clutched my unbuttoned coat around me. The guard spoke into a walkie-talkie: "Zero eight zero, zero two zero, I'm escorting these people to the program room." I assumed he was talking to the guard tower that loomed overhead, letting them know that we were not an escape squad holding a gun on him.

We followed him around the corner of the building into another door, which he opened with a key. Up concrete stairs to another door, also opened with a key. Through a dim, kitchen-like room furnished with stainless steel sinks and tables and smelling faintly and pleasantly of disinfectant. Off to the right and down some stairs, I could see a darkened dining hall. Then through another locked door and down a corridor to the program room.

The guard unlocked the door, switched on a light, and escorted us inside. It was a large, empty, windowless room, freezing cold, painted yellow and white. To the left of the door was a slightly raised platform with a lectern; folded metal chairs leaned against the wall opposite the door.

With a great clanking in the bare, silent room, we set up chairs for ourselves, arranging them in a semicircle in the middle of the floor, and sat wrapped in our coats, waiting for the bridegroom. I envied Divina the warmth of her lamb's-wool turtleneck dress and knee-high boots, and thought longingly of the fuzzy pink sweater I could have worn instead of the linen blouse I'd bought especially for this occasion. With no music to listen to, no arriving guests to observe, no flowered altar to admire, the minutes went by slowly and silently. Then the door opened with a clang, and the groom's party entered: Carlos, two guards, and two inmates, one carrying a large Polaroid camera.

Carlos had the typical bridegroom's face, both nervous and happy, and he was flushed red as a plum. He wore a white brocade shirt with a mandarin collar and black tuxedo pants. One of the guards carried the matching jacket and handed it to Carlos after they entered the room. (Although inmates were not allowed to wear jackets, a special dispensation was given for the ceremony.) When he put on the broad-shouldered bolero jacket, Carlos looked like a blushing matador.

Mirta jumped up the moment Carlos entered the room, and they embraced and kissed. Then she rubbed at his face with a motherly critical finger as if she spotted something amiss. The rest of us remained seated, and Carlos greeted us one by one, moving from chair to chair. When he came to me at the end, he bent down to embrace me. "Linda, I'm so happy to see you."

We shed our coats, leaving them on the chairs, and stood up for the ceremony in an informal circle around the bride and groom. Gabriel, the inmate without a camera, was Carlos's best man and stood next to him. He was taller than Carlos and wore the prison uniform of black shirt and blue jeans, as did the inmate-photographer, a lifer who earned pocket money by taking pictures. He was in prison for murdering his wife, I learned later.

Carlos and Evelin stood facing each other, holding hands. I was to Evelin's left and a little behind her, so I saw her in profile and Carlos straight on. Divina was next to me, holding two typewritten sheets with the Spanish wedding ceremony. Before she began, she asked me for a tissue. "I'm the one who's supposed to cry," I whispered as she dabbed at her eyes.

Octavio and Mirta stood on the other side of Carlos and Evelin, along with the photographer. The three guards discreetly retired to the corner of the room, behind the lectern.

As Divina read the words, I could tell it was much like the traditional ceremony in English. Her voice slowed down as she spoke a phrase that I recognized: "*en prosperidad como en la adversidad.*" When Carlos and Evelin repeated their vows, I knew what they were saying:

"*Yo, Carlos, te recibo a ti Evelin para ser mi esposa desde hoy en adelante para tenerte y conservarte en las alegrías y en las penas. En la riqueza y en la pobreza, en la salud y en la enfermedad para amarte y cuidarte hasta que Dios lo permita. Este es mi voto solemne.*"

"*Yo, Evelin, te recibo a ti Carlos...*"

Octavio presented the box holding two plain gold rings, and Carlos and Evelin slipped them on each other: "*Te doy este anillo como símbolo de mis votos y con todo lo que soy y con todo lo que tengo, yo te honro.*"

Carlos leaned forward and kissed Evelin, who laughed and said, "*No termino*," and we all laughed at the eager groom rushing ahead to his nuptial kiss.

As Divina resumed the ceremony, I glanced over at the guards in the corner. All three of them were staring at me, as if perplexed by my presence. I met their eyes for only a moment and then looked back to Carlos and Evelin.

Divina was blessing their union: "*...Carlos y Evelin se han unido el uno al otro por medio de votos solemnes, con la unión de las manos y on la entrega y recepción de anillos, yo con la autorización que se me ha otorgado le declaro esposo y esposa. Dios los bendiga.*"

"*Ahora*," Evelin smiled, and she and Carlos exchanged a tender kiss. For better or for worse, in happiness or in hardship, they were now married.

Throughout the ceremony and afterwards the photographer's camera whirred, ejecting black rectangles. For one shot I stood against the wall with Carlos and Evelin and Gabriel for the traditional photo of the bride and groom, best man and maid of honor. Gabriel and I were drab attendants, he in his prison uniform, I in my nunlike outfit.

Evelin examined the Polaroids — the joy of instant photography — and exclaimed "*Que lindo!*" at the shot of her hands and Carlos's as they exchanged rings.

Our time in the program room was over, and we had to leave. Carlos, Gabriel, and the photographer would join us downstairs in the visitors' room, where we could continue our celebration. With our coats back on, we non-inmates in the wedding party retraced our steps: back into the freezing prison yard, around the corner, into the little vestibule, and through another door into the visitors' lounge.

The final wedding photos were taken in the children's room, a carpeted, glass-walled corner of the lounge. Carlos and Evelin posed in front of its wall-sized mural of Snow White and the Seven Dwarfs cavorting in the woods with small animals. The bride and groom were now a matching pair of white torsos, Carlos's jacket having been taken from him upstairs. We admired the picture as it developed, and Carlos said, "Take one for Linda, too."

(That photograph now sits in a green-enamel frame on a table in my bedroom. The bride and groom are positioned so that they hide Snow White's entire figure, except for a hand holding up her skirt. That hand projects out behind Evelin's back, as if belonging to an attendant who carries the bride's train. Above their heads you see the dwarfs' thatched cottage nestled in the trees.)

The picture-taking over, we all sat down in the visitors' lounge, a large version of the prison anteroom, with several rows of bus-station chairs and two guards' tables, one on each side of the room. We sat opposite each other, four and three, as if in a railway compartment. Most of the inmates in the room looked like mild, ordinary people who could have been waiting with their families for a bus to arrive or depart.

Octavio and I fetched drinks from the vending machine — Orange Crush and Seven-Up — and we drank a toast to the bride and groom, leaning forward from our facing seats to touch the plastic cups together. Several of Carlos's friends came over to congratulate him, and he laughed as he shook their hands, speaking rapidly in Spanish.

After another round of drinks and another toast, Divina opened up her marriage-record book, and Gabriel and I signed as witnesses. My hand shook a bit as I wrote my name. It seemed a momentous act.

Carlos sat to Evelin's left, with his head against hers and his right arm around her shoulder. His left hand, now wearing a plain gold band, caressed hers. His long, slender fingers never stopped moving across her hand, touching the ring as if it were not plain gold but a priceless and delicate jewel.

At 8:30 we rose to leave; visiting hours were almost over. We retrieved our coats from the rack near the guards' table and said goodbye to Carlos. "Thank you so much for coming," he said to me. After embracing everyone, he clung to Evelin for a long moment, and then walked away from us without looking back. I watched as he strode purposefully toward the door marked "Inmates Only," his retreating back eloquent with determined dignity.

In the prison anteroom Mirta stood by herself, her back turned to us. Her right hand was raised to her brow, covering her eyes, and her shoulders shook. Barely managing to control my own tears, I put my hand on her shoulder to offer comfort but said nothing.

Divina and I reached the car first, and as we waited, I said, "This is so sad, and all because a corrupt cop framed him."

"Oh, that's what happened," Divina said. "I was wondering."

"You don't know the story?" I asked. "Well, I have to tell you." I climbed into the back seat between her and Octavio, and during the long drive back to Boston, Divina and I talked as the others remained silent.

"Carlos is a very lucky young man," Divina said when I finished. "A very lucky young man."

thirteen

MY LAWYER FRIEND JIM HAMILTON had been gleeful when he called me after reading the news about LaFontaine's suspension. "You look like a heroine," he chortled. "As only happens in fairy tales, you are proved absolutely right. It has all the makings of a fabulous story."

"Well, I hope it has a fairy-tale ending. Carlos is still in prison."

"The prosecutor should reopen the case herself," Jim asserted, "but that takes a global sense of integrity and the courage to stand by it."

"Gary Crossen says that's not her job; her job is to protect convictions. Maybe she'll surprise us, but I'm not counting on it."

I was counting instead on the private investigators we were hiring, based on Gary's recommendation. On Valentine's Day, a week after Carlos and Evelin's wedding, I met them for the first time. Joe McCain and Gerry Belliveau sat across the table from Ed and me in a conference room at Foley, Hoag. We had been escorted there by Gary's secretary and now waited for him to arrive. Mike was not able to join us that day.

McCain, a tall man with light hair and blue eyes, was the archetype of an Irish cop even though he was wearing a tweedy sports jacket. He eyed me quizzically, and I returned his skeptical gaze. Was he the right man to get Carlos out of prison?

When Gary arrived a few minutes later, he introduced the detectives. McCain was a former police officer who had been shot in the stomach ten years before by a drug dealer and nearly died. Forced to retire but too active to just sit around, he had become a private detective. Gerry Belliveau, his partner, was a former Secret Service agent and still looked like one in his dark suit. He was shorter and younger than Joe, with thick brown hair and a round face.

Gary had already briefed Joe and Gerry on the case. "I asked them if they felt comfortable as former law enforcement officers in taking a case that involves investigation of a police officer. They said that was no problem." I told the detectives what Blair's contact in the police department had told him about LaFontaine, and the street talk that had been borne out by the current charges against him.

The lawyers were working pro bono, Gary said, but the detectives would be paid at their regular hourly rate. I chimed in to say that I would be the person responsible for paying them, and I was already raising money. We agreed to reassess at the $1,000-$1,500 point.

I told the two detectives about the trial. Joe, who was sitting directly across from me, listened intently, and then asked, "Why did you see things so differently from the rest of the jurors? You say they were biased."

"I'll never understand why I was the only one to smell a rat, Joe. That will always be a mystery to me." He nodded, and I went on. "I thought it was an implausible story told by a witness who was not credible. It just didn't make sense to me, and my instinct told me Carlos was telling the truth and LaFontaine was lying."

"But the others believed him," Joe commented.

"Yes, they believed him. They wanted to believe him."

"Why do you think LaFontaine did it?" Joe asked.

"Maybe at first he really believed it was Carlos he saw that night, but he fudged evidence to make his case stronger. By the time of the trial, he must have known he had the wrong man, but he had promised to send Carlos to prison. Just to make sure, to make Carlos look guilty, he tried to get him to run away."

Joe was incredulous. "He tried to make Carlos run away?"

"Yes, at the first trial he actually told Carlos, 'It's going badly for you. You are going to prison. You'd better run away.' And Carlos almost did. Then before the second trial he told Carlos they had Pablo Osario in jail and had made a deal with him. He said it in Spanish — that's part of his power trip. He can say things in Spanish to Carlos, and other people don't know what he's saying."

When I repeated LaFontaine's admission to Evelin that he might be mistaken, all four men were amazed. "He said that to her!" Joe exclaimed.

What to pursue in the investigation? Finding Pablo was crucial. He must have told the prosecution something they didn't want to hear, or they would have put him on the stand. Also crucial — getting into the building and checking out the details of LaFontaine's story. "I don't think LaFontaine could possibly have seen what he says he did," I said. "And that story about the three black males sounded really fishy to me."

Joe also thought we should check out Carlos's background, and I concurred. "I doubt you'll find anything, but we don't want any surprises." (And indeed they found nothing on Carlos.)

Gary asked how long it would take the detectives to gather new evidence, and Joe estimated at least a month. "I hope we can work quickly on this," I said. "Carlos is suffering terribly."

Joe grimaced. "If you've been around the prison system, you know that you don't want to spend one day in there."

At the end of the hour, I brought up a final point that was much on my mind. "I probably don't need to say this, but I want to keep my name out of this investigation. LaFontaine knows I was helping Blair, but I don't know if he knows my name."

Joe looked concerned and asked if I had talked to anyone in the police department other than Blair's contact. No, I had never even talked to the contact; all that I knew was what Blair had repeated to me.

"Good. Don't talk to anyone there," Joe cautioned.

By now the quality of the eye contact between Joe and me had completely changed. I saw him as an ally, a tough, wounded warrior with a heart. I did not really connect with Gerry Belliveau at that first meeting, but as it turned out, he was the one who handled our case. I never saw Joe McCain again.

"What if you get this guy out and he murders someone?" David the banker asked a few nights later while he was preparing dinner for me.

The question stunned me even though I realized it was the inevitable legacy of Norman Mailer and Jack Abbott: liberal frees convict who promptly kills someone. But I had not expected the question from David. Since the news in January about LaFontaine's suspension, he had seemed much more supportive of my cause. He had even told me that if he ever got in trouble, he'd want me right there in the foxhole with him.

"That won't happen; Carlos is not a murderer," I answered rather lamely, feeling squashed by disappointment. I had been telling David about the meeting with the detectives as I sat on a stool in his kitchen watching him cook. We talked about something else for a while, and then I said, "Oh, I haven't told you about the wedding."

David cut me off. "I don't want to hear any more about Carlos."

I was taken aback by his sharp impatience but immediately apologized. "I'm sorry. I've been boring you with all this talk."

"You don't seem to think about much else," he agreed.

When he walked me home that evening, we parted with a good-night kiss and a promise from me to invite him soon to my place for dinner. He had cooked for me several times, but in spite of much talk about it, I had never reciprocated. I felt that the ball was now in my court, that he would wait to hear from me. But I did not call him, nor did he call me, and that was our last date. Our relationship may never have gotten off the ground anyway, but my preoccupation with Carlos was a clear stumbling block. It was never openly stated, but I felt that I had to choose between David and Carlos. And in that, I had no choice.

I did not know then that the love of my life was waiting in the wings, a man I never would have met if not for the train of events that began with my jury duty.

Two weeks after that first meeting with the detectives, I called the office of Belliveau and McCain and was put through to

Gerry Belliveau. He had just read the transcript over the weekend and had been struck by the sloppy police work. "As a cop I know that's not the way they're trained." When I called back two weeks later, Belliveau had little to add. They were finding it hard to get information off the record because of a current police scandal case. "It's bad timing," Belliveau said. "Everyone is clamming up."

I was discouraged by the slow pace of the investigation; the estimated month for gathering new evidence had passed with nothing in hand. Feeling rather downhearted, I tried to lose myself in the reruns of *Jewel in the Crown* playing nightly on a local UHF station. Although I was mesmerized, it was not the escape I had hoped for.

This second time around, I saw Ronald Merrick, the sadistic police officer, as LaFontaine, and Hari Kumar, his cocky but innocent victim, as Carlos. In episode two, a scene between them roused me to speak aloud as if I were there with them.

Hari is in jail, where he has been brutally interrogated by Merrick. He lies handcuffed on a cot in his cell. Merrick comes in, carrying a metal cup.

"You want a drink?" he asks. Hari drinks thirstily, and then Merrick pulls the cup away.

"There is no love, no justice," he says. "Only power and fear.... Drink if you'll admit it." And Hari gulps the water.

"No!" I shouted to the television screen, to Merrick, to LaFontaine. "There *is* love and justice in the world. I know it, I know it." Then my fierceness gave way to tears. Of love, I was certain, but justice?

My mother was worried that LaFontaine would take revenge on me. I was uneasy myself but tried to calm her fears. "He's a coward, Mother. He only picks on people who can't defend themselves. He's not going to come to Beacon Hill after me." But the banging of a shutter in the night, or the creaking of a wooden desk, woke me with a pounding heart.

One day I thought I saw him on the street, a small, dark-haired man who seemed to be pointing out the bookstore to his companion. "That's where she works," I imagined him saying. When the two men walked on, I trembled with relief. But would he return, to throw acid in my face or slash it with a razor? I knew these fears were irrational. It was not the real man who frightened me, but the symbol of evil he had become. When I actually saw him again, I was astonished that he looked so insignificant.

"LaFontaine's story is a pack of lies," Gerry Belliveau said to the group gathered in a Foley, Hoag conference room: Gary Crossen, Mike Keating, Ed DeMore, and me. It was mid-April, and we were hearing our first report of substance since hiring Belliveau two months before. After weeks of trying to contact the new owners of 223 Geneva Avenue, he had finally succeeded. In early April, he spent a day and a half at the alleged crime scene, inspecting the building (now under renovation), taking pictures, and interviewing tenants.

"A pack of lies," he repeated, pointing to the photographs spread out on the table. "LaFontaine could not possibly have seen into the third-floor apartment from the second-floor landing. The bottom of the staircase gets in the way." On the landing between the second and third floor, he said, you could see the apartment door but not inside the apartment. There was barely enough room for three people on the landing, and they would have blocked the view of anyone behind the door. "There's no way you could get a full view, and he would have been spotted right away."

The kitchen window that LaFontaine said was open from the top actually slid back and forth, not up and down. "That's a major discrepancy," Belliveau said. Having read the transcript carefully, he was familiar with LaFontaine's testimony.

Using a Spanish-speaking interpreter, he interviewed tenants who had lived in the project at the time of the incident. Contrary to the well-lit conditions LaFontaine described, one man said it was so dark that he carried a flashlight and a baseball bat when he went to his car at night. He recognized Pablo Osario immediately when shown his picture, as did eight other longtime tenants. None of them had ever seen Carlos.

Two of the photographs showed the rear of the building. "There's no way someone could jump from the third-floor window without hurting himself, especially with bare feet," Belliveau said. "And it would be very difficult for a man as small as Carlos to get up to the roof from that window. There's an overhang and no ledge. Frankly, I don't think there was anybody in the apartment. There's no way anyone could have gotten out."

"But the description of a suspect in red underwear was in the incident report before Carlos was arrested," I said.

"How do you know when that was written?" Gary Crossen quickly asked.

"You're right," I acknowledged. "I was making an assumption."

Gary stood up to inspect the photographs spread out on the table, lifting them one by one. Then he sat down, shaking his head. "Why Carlos?"

"He was just another Hispanic with gold chains," Belliveau suggested.

"No," Gary said, "there must be a reason. You don't just pick someone off the street and frame them. Maybe there was a woman involved." (Not a bad hunch, as it turned out.)

Mike Keating had been listening with his brow furrowed into nesting chevrons. "How did they know this guy they picked up didn't have a rock-solid alibi?"

"Carlos thought he did," I said.

Unfortunately, the physical evidence that lay before us on the table was not enough to reopen the case because it was discoverable at the time of the trial. It could have been presented then if Carlos had had the resources to hire a detective himself or if Blair had insisted on a more thorough site visit. But this *plus* a statement from Pablo Osario could be the basis for a solid motion for a new trial. Pablo was our best hope, and Belliveau would concentrate on finding him.

Gary had called Lynn Beland to tell her they were reviewing the case. She told him that she was convinced of Carlos's guilt but would be happy to talk to him. "Lynn would never close her eyes," Gary told us.

"Here's a chance for the prosecution to look good," I said. "They can show that they care about justice, not just getting convictions." (This was a common criticism of the Suffolk County D.A.'s office.)

"That's not the way they work," Gary said again. "Their job is to protect convictions." Even tainted ones, it seemed.

Carlos was on an emotional roller coaster — despair and hope and despair again, in an endless round. The INS had quickly slapped a detainer on him, which meant he could not be transferred to a minimum-security prison without permission from Immigration, which was unlikely. Early in January his prison social worker informed him that because of his mandatory sentence he would have to serve three full years in prison, not just one, as he had first been told. That news shattered Carlos's hope of getting out the next fall and starting a new life with his family. "They're taking my dreams away," he sobbed to Evelin.

"He mustn't lose hope," I told her. "If he does, then LaFontaine has won."

When LaFontaine was suspended, late in January, Carlos was elated. He almost expected his cell door to open. He did not know that a jury's verdict is as good as set in stone. Days and weeks went by, and he still waited, not understanding.

Carlos and Evelin now had two baby sons. The second, named Neftalee after Carlos's brother, was born on January 2 and looked just like the other one, Evelin said, except bigger. In late February little Carlos began to walk. A few days later, Evelin made her usual weekend visit to the prison, taking both babies with her. Afterwards she told me all about it.

Carlos cuddled his sleeping two-month-old son, gently rocking him. Little Carlos clung to his father's knees, looking up at him, not sure about the small usurper. Then he turned away, resting a hand on his father's knee before charging off to flaunt his new-found talent for walking.

"Look at him," Evelin said, smiling. "He thinks he's a big shot."

Carlos laughed as he watched his son lurch toward the vending machines at the other end of the room. "That's the cutest thing I ever saw." Then tears filled his eyes. "And I won't be there to see it. I hope I'm there for the little one."

The other inmates were telling Carlos that Evelin would never wait three years for him. "She'll find someone else and stop coming to see you." They were undoubtedly speaking from bitter personal experience, and also out of jealousy, but their words fanned Carlos's own fears. Although Evelin made the long drive to visit Carlos on both Saturday and Sunday every weekend, he still felt miserably insecure.

Three weeks after the wedding, Carlos had told Evelin, "Let's get a divorce. I know you're going to leave me anyway." Evelin was distraught when she told me about it. "He's so insecure, he cries so much. I'm afraid he's going to have a nervous breakdown. He says to me, 'Are you trying to say I'm crazy?' I put myself in the lion's mouth. Fighting, fighting, fighting — whatever I say is wrong." Carlos soon changed his tune, telling her that when he got out of prison, he'd show her off to the world as his wife and treat her the way she had always wanted to be treated. But his insecurity remained.

"It wouldn't be so awful being here if I'd done it," he said to Evelin one Sunday in March as they sat in the babble of the visitors' lounge. "And I was cheated out of my right to defend myself. I never got to tell my story."

"You'll get your chance with the new lawyer," Evelin said.

"But is he going to do anything? If I know for sure something is going to happen, I can wait patiently. Otherwise, I'll go crazy."

Another inmate approached them, a blonde, muscular man with tattooed arms. He accused Carlos of putting a lighted cigarette in his locker. "I know it was you, and you're gonna pay."

Carlos, standing up to leave, said to his friends, "Watch my back."

Evelin cried all night, terrified at what might happen to him, knowing that the guards would let them fight. But Carlos was not harmed. His friends protected him.

Day after day he called her at work, saying, "Take time off. I need to talk to someone. I don't belong here. I don't belong here." The good news about the private detective's visit to the site cheered him for a while, but soon he was down again. He was afraid that lawyers working for free would not do anything. "And I know you're going to leave me," he said. "I'm going to lose everything."

By May, after all this emotion and uncertainty, working full-time and taking care of her family alone, Evelin was deeply discouraged and very tired. The doctor said she was under too much stress. Her home phone was disconnected because she could not pay the monthly bills from Carlos's collect calls. She rarely took his calls at work, for fear of losing her job, and he felt cut off and abandoned. My mother had more sympathy for Evelin than for Carlos. "He sounds like a big baby," she said. (But she had once told me that most men were just great big babies.) "Doesn't he know he's making it harder for her?" I could see Mother's point, but my heart went out to both of them.

Carlos's appeal, an automatic process six months after conviction, was coming up on May 11. (The appeal was a pro forma thing, Gary told me, with only one in a hundred allowed.) Another inmate had recently gone in for an appeal and been freed. "Will that happen to me?" Carlos asked Evelin. "No, honey," she told him, "you can't think like that."

Carlos went into court that day under the mistaken impression that he would meet Gary Crossen and a motion for a new trial would be filed. But instead it was only Warren Blair, still counsel of record. Blair had done nothing on the appeal because he was afraid that Carlos would end up with even more time, since the judge had not sentenced him on the gun charge. Blair made matters worse when he told Carlos not to count on Gary. "Nothing's going to happen. No one does anything for free. He's not going to do anything; he's just doing a favor for a friend of a friend."

"It's all a game," Carlos said to Evelin. "I don't believe anything."

"Our hopes went down the tubes," Evelin told me. "If it's a question of money, Carlos's mother will take a loan on her house."

I tried to reassure her. "It's not a question of money. Warren is wrong — Gary is working very hard on this case. And things are happening, but he made me promise not to say anything yet."

What I could not tell her was that Gerry Belliveau and Gary Crossen had just found Pablo Osario.

fourteen

FINDING PABLO'S ADDRESS HAD BEEN simple. Gerry Belliveau checked with the Registry of Motor Vehicles and learned that Pablo had recently renewed his driver's license. Finding Pablo himself was not so simple. I envisioned the scene as it was described to Ed, Mike, and me in our usual conference room at Foley, Hoag.

Gary Crossen and Gerry Belliveau, both wearing suits and looking like federal agents, enter a seedy, triple-decker apartment building in Brockton, Massachusetts. They knock on a door. No one answers, but several other doors open and heads pop out to look at them. Then the doors slam.

"I should get hazardous duty pay for this," Gary says. "Oh, I forgot to ask. Are you packing?" he asks Belliveau.

"No, I left my gun in the trunk," the detective replies sheepishly.

"Great. And I don't have my running shoes on."

They walk up another flight and knock on several more doors. Two or three are opened by people who shake their heads as Gary speaks to them. Finally, an older woman, standing in her doorway, gesticulates as she describes where to find Pablo.

Change of scene: A cabinetmaker's shop. The noise of saws and sanders, dust in the air. Gary and Belliveau talk to the foreman, who points toward a man using an electric sander on a bureau. He is tall and thin, with short hair and tortoise-shell glasses. It is Pablo Osario. He looks up as the two men approach, listens as Gary says something to him, and then all three men leave the shop. Outside, near a windowless wall, they begin to talk. Pablo lights a cigarette.

"He spoke halting English and was obviously nervous," Gary said. "His hands were trembling and his voice shaking." Pablo told them that LaFontaine arrested him for cocaine trafficking at 223 Geneva Avenue and took his license from his wallet; later Pablo learned that LaFontaine filed a report saying the license was found in apartment 3E. "Pablo volunteered that, without any prompting from us," Gary said. "That backs up Carlos's story."

Pablo and his brother-in-law had formerly lived in 3E, but at the time of his arrest Pablo was living on the first floor with a friend named Carmen. Pablo denied that either he or his brother-in-law distributed cocaine. He had been in the parking lot the night of the incident and saw officers come out of the building.

After his arrest on the drug charge, Pablo spent several months in jail before he could make bail. When he was released he returned to the Geneva Avenue project for his belongings. LaFontaine saw him there and beat him up, arresting him afterwards for assault and battery on a police officer. Belliveau showed us the mug shot taken after Pablo's arrest; his bruised face was swollen like a melon. Pablo was given six months' probation for that charge.

Pablo looked at a picture of Carlos. He had never seen him, he said; he had never even heard of Carlos before their indictment in this case. Somehow Pablo had not been prosecuted for the cocaine trafficking charge, and he thought the warrant had been recalled. Gary advised Pablo to get in touch with his court-appointed attorney, because records showed an outstanding arrest warrant.

Both Gary and Belliveau found Pablo to be credible. The best news of all: he was willing to sign an affidavit for us. "He was extremely, surprisingly cooperative," Gary concluded.

"Why didn't they prosecute Pablo on the drug charge, and how did he get out of jail last September?" Mike wondered. We knew from our investigation that Pablo had indeed been in jail in September, as LaFontaine had told Carlos.

"And what about the deal LaFontaine said they made with Pablo to testify against Carlos?" I asked.

"Pablo says he never talked to LaFontaine in jail," Gary answered.

"So the bastard made the whole thing up," I said in disgust.

The next step was to get an affidavit from Pablo, with his lawyer's permission. Pablo's testimony, and the parallels between his arrest and Carlos's, would be new evidence, perhaps enough to get a motion over the transom. But Gary cautioned us. "We've got to get it right. Remember, we're only going in there once."

Four days after that meeting, on May 16, the unrelated case against LaFontaine moved ahead. A judge in Dorchester District Court heard testimony against LaFontaine and his partner and found probable cause for criminal charges against them. "District Judge Lawrence Shubow heard from 11

witnesses during three days of testimony," Sean Murphy reported in the *Boston Globe* the next day. "In 36 years as a lawyer and
judge," Shubow said, "I've never seen such dramatic support
for the contention that police officers were off on some kind of
caper of their own." LaFontaine was charged with larceny, two
counts of indecent assault, and two counts of attempted extortion; Pomales, with larceny and two counts of attempted extortion. Their case would now go to the Suffolk County grand jury.

Denying all the charges, LaFontaine and Pomales had giv-
en their version of what happened, which the *Globe* recounted:
They were tipped off to drug dealing at 238 Columbia Road by
a woman who stopped them on the street as they patrolled in
plainclothes. About thirty minutes later, they spotted a man, later identified as Joseph Taylor, who fit the description, and they
attempted to buy cocaine from him. "Taylor took about $1,000
in cash from the officers and led them to the apartment, where
about 10 people were assembled in the living room, including
one who apparently recognized LaFontaine and called out 'the
cops are here,' according to the officers' testimony."

LaFontaine testified that he disarmed Joseph Taylor of a
.38-caliber revolver as he reached for it in his belt, and Taylor
admitted to owning 48 grams of cocaine found in the apartment. None of the females was searched or even patted down,
the officer said.

The occupants of the apartment testified to a very different story: LaFontaine and Pomales arrived at the apartment
without a warrant at about midnight and searched for drugs.
"When the officers found cocaine and marijuana, they handcuffed Howard Taylor and Joseph Taylor and said it would 'cost
$5,000 apiece' for the officers to release the men, according to
testimony.

"While the group pooled the money, LaFontaine took Alves, who is in her early 20s, into the bedroom alone, assaulted her and indicated that he wanted sex 'to help her friends,' according to her testimony. He later took Linda Taylor, Howard's sister, into the bathroom and made the same indication, according to testimony."

When LaFontaine and Pomales could collect only $4,800, they arrested Joseph Taylor, saying charges against him could be dropped later in exchange for the outstanding $5,200. After the two officers left the apartment, Howard Taylor called a local politician, who contacted the police. Within hours, members of the Boston police anti-corruption unit began interviewing witnesses, Taylor said.

"The two officers said they were in the apartment about 90 minutes, but radio transmissions showed they were there for about three hours, according to testimony."

Frank McGee, the defense attorney for the two officers, said, "This is a case that comes down to credibility. It's whether you believe those who were found in an apartment where a significant drug operation was located, or do you believe the police?" The assistant D.A. in the case admitted that his witnesses were "no Boy Scouts, no citizens of the year, but the travesty is that's exactly why these police officers thought they could get away with this."

LaFontaine scoffed at the charges. "We did nothing. It's all ridiculous," he said.

A follow-up piece the next day, also written by Sean Murphy, ran with the headline "Officer accused of shakedown has long history of complaints." Some details from that story were later incorporated into Carlos's motion for a new trial.

"Albert LaFontaine, one of two police officers charged with extorting money and sex from two alleged drug dealers and their girlfriends, has faced dozens of accusations of criminal behavior and misconduct during his 15-year police career. LaFontaine, 45, of Brockton, was suspended from duty without pay for one year [seven years before Carlos's trial] after a judge found sufficient facts for a guilty finding against him on an assault and battery charge. The assault occurred in a cell at the West Roxbury District Court, according to records obtained by The Boston Globe. When the victim's attorney tried to stop the beating, LaFontaine arrested the lawyer for disorderly conduct. In another incident, the city [four years before Carlos's trial] paid $9,000 to settle a civil rights suit brought by a man who claimed to have been severely beaten by LaFontaine in a police station jail cell.

"LaFontaine was the subject of at least 27 internal police department investigations for brutality or other acts of misconduct [in an eight-year period], according to an affidavit filed in U.S. District Court. He was fired as a police officer [four years before Carlos's trial] for misconduct in allegedly operating a second-hand jewelry store in Jamaica Plain while on leave from the department due to an injury. LaFontaine was accused of lying to superior officers about the business, which police officers are prohibited from operating, and violated department rules against working while on leave. But the state Civil Service Commission voted 5-0 to reverse LaFontaine's termination and awarded him back pay."

After reprising the current charges against LaFontaine, the story went on: "LaFontaine and his lawyer, Frank J. McGee, Jr., could not be reached for comment yesterday. Police sources who are familiar with LaFontaine portrayed him as being constantly in trouble with superior officers."

It was clear from this story that by the time LaFontaine testified against Carlos, the police department had ample evidence that he was a rogue officer — brutal, lawless, and untruthful. Yet he was allowed to go on the stand as a credible witness, with the power to ruin a life.

7 June

Hello, dear Linda!!

Reason of this letter is to say hi to you and giveing you my thanks for everything you did for me. I'm very happy for what your doing for me out there. Now that you are the only person that know the hole true about my problems that hurting my mind and my thoughts.

Since the day they sentence me, my live has change all around and I seen a lot of crazy things in here. I hope in the future it doesn't bring me bad memory because this has been too much for me. I very happy that there still good people out there haven't forgot about me especialy my wife and my sons and you that have been something special in my life. I pray God that nothing change untill the end of this bad time I'm going thru right now.

Dear friend, since your the only person that know all the damage that these people did to me I ask you if you see that it inposible for me plese let me know ahead of time. That way I won't be thinking the way I'm doing. Because every day that goes bye I hope that I'm going to get good news but the way I see thing it just ilusion so that way my mind won't suffer. I don't know why I'm going thru this because in my heart and my mind is nothing hiding about this case.

I'm not forsing you to get me out of here I just want you to explain to me what going on or explain to my family what going on because they are the only person that I can count on these moments and you know that those people are my wife and kids

*that I need this moment so sad. Whatever hapens, when I get out
of here even if it is three years or if I'm luckie to get out before that
I would look for a way to pay you back for everything you have
done for me because I'm very thankfull of you and a lot of people
that knows the true and I'm not the man who did all this and they
accuse me.*

God bless you all your life Linda.

love, Carlos Montilla

On Father's Day, a week or so after receiving Carlos's letter,
I went to visit him with Evelin and little Carlos, now eighteen
months old; only three visitors were allowed at a time, including children. On the drive down, I read the letter aloud. Evelin
wiped away tears and then glanced at little Carlos asleep in the
back seat. "He misses his father so much," she said sadly.

On weekends in warm weather inmates received their visitors outside in a small park, where roses grew on trellises against
the prison walls. Evelin and I chose a bench under a tree, in
sun-dappled shade. It was a hot day, but a lovely breeze stirred
the leaves. "There he is," Evelin said, and I saw Carlos walking
toward us from the prison door. His gait was now familiar to me
— smooth and fluid, with just a hint of a strut. He was wearing
a black short-sleeved shirt and jeans, the required prison garb.
Even at a distance, I could see the pleased, shy smile on his face.

"Look who's coming," Evelin said to little Carlos, whom I
was holding. When he spotted his father, he pulled away from
me, holding out his arms. "You can put him down," Evelin said,
and when I did, he toddled off toward Carlos, who scooped him
up. After Evelin and I got drinks and chips from the vending
machine inside, we sat down on the bench. It was like a typical
Sunday in the park, enclosed by a chain-link fence.

"You wouldn't know you were in prison," Evelin said.

Carlos nodded toward the building behind us. "If you go inside, you'd know." He then spoke in Spanish to Evelin, who said, "You tell her."

He turned to me and said shyly in English, "I'm glad to see you. Thank you for coming."

"I'm glad to see you, too. I've been meaning to come see you and when I got your letter, I thought this would be a good time." The letter, Carlos explained through Evelin, involved lots of translating back and forth from Spanish to English.

"You'll be glad to hear that one of the lawyers will be coming to talk to you soon," I said. "They're planning to file the motion for a new trial soon, if all goes well. We're hoping for a statement from Pablo Osario, but I can't tell you any more than that. We have to be very careful." Gary had pledged me to silence until Pablo gave us an affidavit. He was afraid of the prison grapevine: "You'd be amazed at how things get out." And Pablo had stood us up several times, pleading that he had to work late. But Belliveau would escort him to Foley, Hoag for the next appointment, coming up in a few days.

"Can you just tell me if we're getting close?" Carlos asked.

"Yes, very close. I'm hopeful, but nothing is guaranteed."

Carlos then told me what his mother and his family were saying to him: God put him in prison so he'd learn about life, but He also put me on the road to get him out.

"They may be right," I laughed. "And I won't give up even if the motion fails. I'll march into the governor's office, and if that doesn't work I'll go to the newspapers."

The conversation turned to LaFontaine, and Evelin told me about an incident at the second trial. In LaFontaine's hearing, she had said, "He's a liar." He was furious and lunged toward her: "I'm not a liar. Tell her to shut up or I don't know what will happen." And Blair told her to keep quiet.

"Well, he's completely discredited now, and I doubt very much they'll try Carlos again if we win the motion. He's their only witness, and he could be in prison himself before long." Then I said to Evelin, "Does Carlos know that if he's tried again, there'll be no jury?"

Evelin explained to Carlos, who looked surprised and relieved. "That's good," he said, "because I think there is discrimination."

"Definitely," I said, touched by his understatement.

Evelin then told me that after the mistrial, a dark-haired fellow came up to her, "the one wearing a suit who acted as if he was running things." I smiled to myself at her description of Aaron, and explained what a foreman was. "Well, he was real mean and told me, 'There are other alternatives.'"

"Meaning that they could still get Carlos, and he was right," I said.

We wondered whether the other jurors had seen the stories about LaFontaine. "I hope they read about LaFontaine and know they made a mistake," Evelin said. "I want them to suffer."

Carlos sat with his right arm around Evelin's shoulders, his left hand stroking hers, which rested on his leg. Their heads were close, or touching, all the time. Little Carlos had been playing with a young girl, about ten years old, who snatched him up shortly after we sat down on the bench. "The same people come every week," Evelin explained. "We all know each other." Now the girl brought him back, saying, "He wants Dada." Little Carlos stood at his father's knees and held out a tiny dandelion as if he were presenting a rare and delicate jewel.

"Is that your Father's Day present?" I asked him.

"A Father's Day present for Poppy?" Carlos repeated, but little Carlos pulled his hand back as if he had second thoughts about parting with his prize, and ran away. He returned shortly, and Carlos took him on his lap, feeding him potato chips from a bag and teasing him in English, "Hungry, hungry, eating so fast."

When he finished the bag of chips, little Carlos looked over and smiled at me, then reached out his arms. "You want to go to Linda?" Carlos asked, setting him down. He clung to my knees and then turned around for a boost up. I cuddled the little boy on my lap as Carlos and Evelin talked together in Spanish.

"Where are you going now?" Carlos asked her. She told him that first she was taking me home and then going to her father's. "Are you sure that's all?" Carlos persisted. "You look so pretty." All this was in Spanish, but Evelin told me about it later in the car, explaining that other inmates still taunted Carlos about Evelin finding another man. "Where's your wife tonight?" they would ask. "Out dancing?" Although some of these men were Carlos's friends, who supported him and protected him, they were very jealous that he had a beautiful wife who visited him regularly.

As we sat there on the bench, she merely said to me, "He's saying I look very pretty."

"You're beautiful," I said, and turning to Carlos, "You're very lucky."

Carlos leaned his head on Evelin's shoulder and said, "I know it." Then he went on in Spanish, which Evelin translated: "I never want to be in prison again. I'll never do anything that might get me in trouble. When I get out, I'll stick to my family like glue."

"Moral of the story: stay at home," I said.

Evelin laughed. "He knows it."

"Carlos, you're going to have to go inside yourself to find strength to get through this. I can't do it for you. Evelin can't do it for you. You must find it inside yourself." I said the words gently but firmly, and Evelin translated for me.

Carlos nodded and replied, "As long as I know I have a chance, I can be calm."

As we prepared to leave, Carlos took little Carlos from me and kissed him again and again on the cheek. When he put him down, the tot ran off toward the inmates' exit in the fence and was halfway to the prison door when Carlos, laughing, caught up with him. We all walked together to the guard's table by the visitors' exit to say goodbye. I hugged Carlos and told him, "Take care of yourself and try not to think too much."

"Thank you for coming," he said. "I'll never forget you."

I laughed. "I'll certainly never forget you either." Then I told them a recent dream: "I was looking down into a deep, bottomless pit lined with slimy stones. Someone I knew had fallen into it. When I woke up, I thought, I know who that was. It was you," I said, putting my hand on his shoulder.

"And you were pulling him out with a rope," Evelin said, imitating the motion, hand over hand, and we all laughed.

At the car, Evelin buckled little Carlos into the infant seat in the back. "Dada?" he asked, and then began to sing happily to himself, keeping it up most of the way home.

"Did you notice how fast he was eating those chips when he was sitting on Carlos's lap?" Evelin asked me. "He never eats like that at home."

"Maybe he's pining away for his father."

"That's what Carlos thinks."

fifteen

PABLO OSARIO WAS MISSING. OUR star witness, our best hope to get a new trial for Carlos, had disappeared.

On July 5 Gerry Belliveau drove down to Brockton to pick up Pablo and take him to Foley, Hoag to sign the affidavit he had given to Gary Crossen and a translator in late June. Pablo was not home, nor was anyone else, and his apartment appeared to be vacant. No one was at the cabinetmaker's shop where Pablo worked; it was closed for the week.

"Find him," Gary told Belliveau. "Check with the landlord to see if the July rent's been paid. If he's moved, get the new address. Whatever you do, find him."

"He might have bolted," Gary told me when he broke the news about our vanished ace in the hole. Had LaFontaine gotten to him? What would we do if we couldn't find him? But Belliveau had his marching orders, and he followed them. He contacted Pablo's landlord and learned that Pablo had moved, but only to a nearby apartment. A few days later Belliveau drove back to Brockton, to the new address, and found Pablo at home.

I imagine the scene as a surprised, bare-footed Pablo opens the door. "You stood me up the other day," Belliveau says with a strained smile, "but you're coming with me now. Put your shoes on." Pablo looks sullen but does not protest. In silence the two men drive back to Boston, to Foley, Hoag, where the crucial document lies on a table, ready for Pablo's signature....Gary points to where Pablo is to sign and hands him a pen. Pablo hesitates, his hand poised above the paper.

On July 11, almost exactly a year after Carlos's first trial began, Pablo Osario, the missing co-defendant, signed an affidavit that was Carlos's best chance of getting out of prison.

I was brimming over with that news when I ran into Paul Horovitz on Charles Street as I was heading back to the store after lunch. A lawyer with an office nearby, Paul was one of our favorite customers, and he had followed the story from the beginning. I told him about Pablo and almost as an afterthought asked if he would like to help with the cost of the detectives.

"Yes, I'd be glad to do that," he replied. "I'm sure it's mounting up." (Indeed it was, and Belliveau had just asked me for payment. More than a dozen people had already contributed or made pledges, but more was needed.)

"Even a token contribution would mean a lot symbolically," I said. "The name of the account is 'Committee for Justice.'"

My first contribution had come a few months before from Mrs. Eacker, an elegant older woman who lived around the corner. Like all of our regular bookstore customers, she had heard the Carlos story from me. When I told her that her neighbor Mike Keating was taking on the case, she was thrilled. "He's the best, you know. But who's paying for all this?" Without waiting for an answer, she said, "I'll give you $100. You can do anything you want with it." Mrs. Eacker's unsolicited gift gave me the courage to ask other people for contributions, and I opened an account at my local bank, calling it "Committee for Justice."

When I told the branch manager what the account was for, she waived the service charge.

Almost everyone I approached for help said yes immediately. A few, like Mrs. Eacker, gave without being asked, earning double gratitude. One friend who was out of work insisted on donating ten dollars, saying, "I wish I could do more, but I want to be part of it." None of these people had met Carlos. They were willing, these generous souls, to help win justice for a stranger. I was deeply heartened by their support, knowing it was for me personally as well as for Carlos. I saw the best in people coming out, like a spreading web of goodness.

But nothing had prepared me for Paul's response to my request. About an hour after our conversation on the street, he came into the bookstore while Sue and I were chatting with a customer. He handed me a folded check, said "Here you are," and walked out. I opened the check and glanced at the amount. At first I thought it said $100, but then I did a double take, unable to believe my eyes: One thousand dollars!

I ran after Paul and caught him in front of the bookstore window. "Paul, you can't do this. I'm completely bowled over."

"But I want to do it. Since the legal system screwed up in putting him in prison, it seems appropriate for someone in the legal system to help get him out."

"But it seems like too much for one person."

"You're not going to tear it up, are you?" He smiled at me, his brown eyes twinkling.

I hesitated. "No, of course not. You're wonderful. I can't thank you enough." With tears in my eyes, I gave him a big hug.

"Now I know the force is with us," I said. "Getting this and hearing about Pablo all on the same day."

The following week Mike Keating took time off from his vacation to visit Carlos in prison, their first meeting. Mike, wearing khakis and a polo shirt, went in alone, without an interpreter. Carlos, very nervous and expecting someone in a suit with slicked-down hair, looked at this casually dressed man and knew immediately that he was someone with a heart, someone important who still had humility, someone who could help him. Mike, expecting to be neutral, instantly saw Carlos's childlike quality. Startled by the unexpected, they saw each other's essence in one keen, heartening glance. They looked at each other in surprise for a moment, and then both men smiled.

That visit to Carlos marked a shift in Mike's involvement in the case. "At first, the intellectual commitment was more important," he said later. "I saw it as a puzzle: here was an injustice and how could we turn it around. But by the end, the emotional commitment was much more important." In the interests of justice, Mike would have kept on with the case even if Carlos had struck him as a hardened criminal or as clever and manipulative, but he wouldn't have put so much of himself into it. By the time we finally went into court, Mike was deeply committed. Before he left his house that morning, this eminent litigator said to his wife, "This may be the most important thing I've ever done."

❧

My fiftieth birthday was coming up on August 6. "It's only a number," I shrugged. But it was a big number and could not be ignored.

"You must be freaking out over turning fifty," one friend said when I announced in June that I was letting my hair grow out to its natural gray.

"I don't think I'm freaking out," I protested. "It doesn't feel that way at all. I'm just ready to be what I am."

My hair had begun to turn gray in my late twenties, and for years I colored it myself with one product or another. When a disaster turned it to straw, I threw in the towel and surrendered to a professional colorist. Now I was not sure what true hair color lay underneath the natural-looking brown, but I had seriously silver roots that demanded fixing every five weeks, and I could only go that long because my hair was thick and wavy. I was a slave to my root line, in thrall to the colorist, but I chaffed under the tyranny. Mutiny was brewing.

Part of the rebellion was my growing uneasiness with the artifice, the unreal surface that hid the truth. The Carlos case had made me think more deeply about appearance and reality, both philosophically and in my own life. I knew I appeared to be younger than my actual age partly because of my dyed hair, and that bothered me. I didn't want to pretend to be something I wasn't.

But even though I squirmed beneath the artifice, the thought of going natural frightened me — not just *being* gray, but *becoming* gray. There seemed to be no graceful way to retreat from the dye pot. And how would I look once the deed was done? Would I be like the actress in *Lost Horizon* who turned from young girl to old crone in just a few frames?

I had been teetering on the brink for months when I went for a touchup in May before a hiking trip in Scotland. (That was part of the tyranny, having to coordinate hair appointments with vacations so as not to sprout gray while in another country.) Already out of sorts because of a scheduling mix-up, I sat wrapped in a plastic cape while the colorist swabbed my root line with brown goo. It was the smell, I think, that pushed me over the line. As the chemicals assaulted my nose, something inside me clicked: I don't want to do this anymore. And I didn't.

"You could gradually go lighter and lighter," my stylist suggested when I told him in June I was finally taking the plunge. But I wanted to be free of the whole coloring routine and went cold turkey instead, getting a shorter haircut each month. Helped by the summer sun, the dye began to fade and the gray blended in. Some people thought I was having my hair streaked. Although the growing out was not as bad as I had expected, I still felt that I was taking a bold step.

Some of my friends were dubious, even disapproving, especially younger women or women my age who colored their hair, but most were encouraging. The finished product that emerged five months later received almost universal affirmation. Amazingly, some people thought that my new silver hair made me look younger.

When I turned fifty, I was only halfway through the growing-out process, but already felt liberated and authentic. This is the real me, I thought with relief. I was no longer a young girl — thank God in many ways — but a mature woman. I was ready for it.

I celebrated my birthday in a series of parties and get-togethers. After a party in Boston, I headed up to Maine for a long weekend and another party. My longtime friend Connie baked a delicious chocolate cake and decorated it with violets from her garden. Connie's husband, Lou, her mother, Gina, Gina's friend Lorraine, and my friend Jane from high school sat around the table in Connie's dining room wearing silly pointed hats and having a wonderful time.

That night I had a vivid dream: In a medieval setting along a river bank, large baskets were being raised and lowered. Then, inside a church, someone who was thought to be dead was alive after all. Medieval musicians with lutes began to play rock and roll. A lone person in the congregation stood up and began to dance. Soon everyone was standing up and dancing, waving their arms.

When I told this dream to Connie the next morning, she looked as if she had seen a ghost. "I had a dream just like that last night." But in her dream, the people in the church were not celebrating, but waving their arms in horror at some holocaust that was happening outside.

"Are you sure they weren't dancing?" I asked.

"I'm sure," she said. "It was very frightening."

When Jane came down for breakfast, we asked her what it meant that Connie and I had such similar dreams on the same night. Jane, a therapist, could not explain it. "All I know is that I feel left out," she said wistfully.

The news that awaited me when I returned to Boston on Tuesday afternoon made me wonder if I had been wrong about what was going on in my dream. Maybe those people weren't dancing after all.

The day before, Gary had been called out of a meeting with an urgent message: "There's a woman in tears on the phone." It was Evelin, almost hysterical. "They're going to deport Carlos right away," she sobbed. Carlos had been ready that day for his requested transfer to a minimum-security prison, which the Department of Correction had recently approved. His clothes were packed, and he was saying goodbye to his friends. Then the guards told him, "Montilla, you're not going anywhere. You have a deportation hearing next week."

Gary tried to calm her down. "Don't be upset. We will take care of it."

When I heard the news from Evelin, I hid my own alarm. A few weeks earlier I had read in the newspaper that alien inmates were being deported to relieve prison overcrowding, but I thought it only applied to illegal aliens. Carlos had a green card; he was a legal resident. Technically, he would be deported after serving his sentence, but that was two years away, and surely by then his conviction would be overturned. However, if he were deported before we could file a motion for a new trial, all our efforts on his behalf would come to nothing.

Gary, when he filled me in, downplayed the crisis. "It's nothing earth-shaking," he said. We would object to the deportation on the grounds that a motion for a new trial would shortly be filed. Gary got in touch with the lawyer covering the case for the INS, who told him Immigration wouldn't back off because of the pending motion. They would fight the continuance that Gary planned to ask for at the hearing. It would be up to the judge, who was coming from Arizona to handle the eighteen cases scheduled for that day.

"Carlos will die," Evelin said, when I told her Gary would ask for a continuance. "He wants to go to minimal so much." But the only alternative to a continuance was deportation.

A day or so before the hearing Gary drove down to Bridgewater to talk to Carlos. They could speak only through a grate and without an interpreter. Although communication was difficult, Carlos made it clear to Gary that he wanted to fight his deportation as vigorously as possible. "I was impressed by him," Gary told me. "He could have taken that opportunity to get out of prison early, but he didn't. That told me that he felt he was in the right."

Terrified at the prospect of being deported and thereby losing his wife and sons (his worst fear), Carlos was reassured when he met Gary and learned he would be at the hearing. Carlos had immediate confidence in him; he liked the way Gary talked, the way he put his lips together. The judge at the hearing on August 18 must also have liked the way Gary talked. Over the strenuous objections of the lawyer for the INS, the judge accepted Gary's arguments and agreed to continue the case until October. The threat had been deflected, at least temporarily. (Later the hearing was postponed indefinitely, deportation fever having apparently subsided.)

Now, after meeting Carlos, Gary also took a more personal interest in the case. He tried to get Carlos reclassified by Immigration so he could be transferred to a minimum-security prison, but the people he talked to there, a judge and an attorney, told him that a transfer was up to the Department of Correction. The prison officials, on the other hand, were telling Carlos that he couldn't be transferred without permission from the INS; he was considered a flight risk because of the deportation threat, and it was easier to escape from a minimum-security prison. Carlos seemed to be stuck in Bridgewater, hung up between the two agencies.

Gary also talked to the parole board, who told him that next September was the earliest that Carlos could be released. Here at last was the answer to how long he would have to serve: two years. I was angry. "Why didn't the prison officials know that?" I asked Gary. "They kept jerking him around. First, it was one year, and then it was three with no chance of parole. Why couldn't they give him a straight answer?"

Gary, of course, could not answer my question. "All I know is that's what the parole board has down for him."

But it was academic, anyway; Carlos would surely be out long before then.

❦

On September 23, LaFontaine and his partner were fired from the police department. Commissioner Roache ordered them dismissed for violating department rules, including conduct unbecoming an officer, searching a female without a female officer present, and failure to report their whereabouts. The decision came after a series of internal hearings to investigate their alleged shakedown of drug dealers. They still faced criminal charges for that incident.

It was unusual for indicted officers to be fired before a case was resolved, and their lawyer complained: "These guys have been fired without first having their full day in court." Clearly, the police department was washing its hands of the two officers.

When I took the newspaper clipping to Gary Drug to be photocopied, Eileen was behind the counter. She knew the Carlos story, having heard it from me months before when she photocopied one of the earlier stories about LaFontaine. She often asked me how things were going and was delighted to see that "the dirty cop" had been fired.

"Why isn't this enough to get that poor guy out of jail?" she asked.

"It just isn't," I answered. "You wouldn't believe how hard it is to overturn a jury's verdict. Even proving someone innocent is not enough."

"That doesn't seem right," she said, shaking her head.

Eileen was not the only one at the drugstore who was following the case. Cristi, another young woman, often joined in my conversations with Eileen, and she too was rooting for Carlos. So was Helena, the young Irishwoman at a Charles Street café who made me a special cappuccino every morning.

"How's your little fellow doing?" she often asked me, sometimes sitting down at the table to listen if I had much to tell her. I was buoyed by the support of these young women and of many other people, some of whom I barely knew.

Staunchest of the allies, of course, were my family and close friends. By phone and in person, they put in their voices, a loyal coterie cheering from the front row. "I'm invested," my friend Jane told me. "I'm in for the long haul." Tom in Vermont called frequently to ask "What's happening?" and seemed crushed if there was no good news to report. My friends who had prayer lists had added Carlos's name.

"A friend like you comes along once in a blue moon" was the printed message on the card Carlos sent me in late September. It was illustrated with a cat on a fence, who is joined by another; a full, blue moon rises behind them. On the blank reverse side of the card Carlos wrote:

> *I have to tell you that I'm very happy knowing that you worry for me. I never stop thinking in all that you have do for me...*
>
> *Linda, listen: on this place I have learn what is life and how to survive and I have realize how much I miss my family and all my love ones, especially my son and wife.*
>
> *Every night before bed time I make a prayer to the Holy God and only power God, asking him to forgive me for all my sings that I have commitid in my life, plus I pray and ask God to give you bless and inteligents every day. Tomorrow and ever.*
>
> *With all my respets and love and care I finish this letter and remember that I will never forgive you.*

I read this aloud to Sue in the bookstore, and we smiled at the errors that made the heartfelt message even more poignant. "I guess we've all committed some 'sings' in our lives," she said, "and maybe 'forgive' and 'forget' are the same in Spanish."

At a dinner party in late October, a neighbor who knew the story about Carlos made a point of talking to me. "You're wasting your time," he said. "The system doesn't work, you know. The money for the private detectives would have been better spent on a well-placed bribe." Struck to the heart, I said nothing, and he went on gleefully, seeming to relish his cynical message. "You need an enforcer, like this big dude I know named Tyrone. Sixteen-inch biceps. I can give you his phone number."

I brooded for days about my neighbor's words. Had I been an idealistic chump to believe that justice and truth would win out? Would a well-placed bribe have brought Carlos home by now? But even if that cynical remark reflected the real world, it completely missed the point of what we were doing. I wouldn't want to get Carlos out by playing the cynic's game. Winning that way would be defeat, not victory. But the disheartening fact remained that Carlos had been in prison for more than a year, and almost certainly would spend another Christmas there.

sixteen

EVELIN HAD GIVEN UP HOPE: "I'm just going to accept whatever happens." Carlos was not talking to her, she said. I admitted that I too was discouraged at how long it was taking. "But I don't want to push to file the motion if we're two days away from getting something important."

After we hung up, I called Gary. "I've had three dreams this week that I'm on a slippery, muddy path," I told him.

"It *is* a slippery, muddy path," he said. "As long as you don't run over me. Was I face down in the mud?"

"No, but I think you may have been in the one last night. There was a scientist making studies on the path."

"A scientist? I'm not a scientist."

"Yes, but you're skeptical like a scientist."

"I am," he admitted. "But when you hear me in court, you'll have no idea of that."

"All right, as long as you do a good job. Your role in this is to be skeptical. My role is to be a believer. I have this drama cast with an innocent man, an evil cop, and white knights, and I'm not going to change it in the middle of the third act."

"As long as I can still be a white knight," Gary said playfully.

"Oh, you're definitely a white knight. I just wish you could make that horse go a little faster."

Overturning a conviction was an uphill battle, Mike said, and what we had was thin. If we could prove that LaFontaine had a motive for framing Carlos it would be a slam dunk. Mike and Gary had delayed finishing the motion for a new trial in the hopes of nailing down the connection between LaFontaine and a woman both he and Carlos knew, a relationship that may have given LaFontaine a motive to frame Carlos, or at least to pursue the case against him.

About the time of his arrest — while he was living with Evelin — Carlos had an affair with a married woman named "Dolores" with two kids. She had pursued Carlos, and in late November, had left her husband for him. Carlos lived with Dolores for about two weeks around Christmas before dumping her and returning to Evelin. "She can't hold a candle to you," he said.

"Why did you do it?" Evelin asked, and he had no answer.

A week after Carlos stopped seeing Dolores, he went to Dorchester Court for a hearing on the charges resulting from his arrest. Carlos was surprised to see Dolores in the hallway and even more surprised by the officer with her: LaFontaine, the man who had arrested him. He watched them conversing and then Dolores suddenly yelled out, "Carlos, you're going to prison for three years!" She laughed and laughed. Dolores was in the courthouse to press charges against her husband for kidnapping their son. Later Carlos heard through his cousin that LaFontaine had vowed to ruin Carlos's life because he had broken up Dolores's marriage. But Carlos didn't believe it and never told Blair.

The connection between LaFontaine, Dolores, and Carlos — like the physical layout of the scene — was not technically new evidence, being discoverable at the time of the trial. But according to state case law, it could be added on to tip the scale if it was presented along with new evidence not discoverable at the time of the trial. (Fortunately, we were not in Texas, where any new evidence had to be presented within thirty days of conviction.) In our case, that new evidence was Pablo's affidavit and the revelations of LaFontaine's misconduct. The officer's record was even more blemished now that he and his partner had been fired from the police department.

Any prior knowledge of Carlos by LaFontaine would be a significant non-disclosure, enough to raise serious concerns and give the motion more weight than would be expected in such a case. But first we must substantiate the connection, and that was like trying to catch a fish with bare hands.

We hired a Spanish-speaking investigator who tracked down Dolores in the middle of August and interviewed her. She denied knowing LaFontaine, saying she had never heard of him. "This is old history," she said about her affair with Carlos. She knew Carlos was in jail and told the investigator, "He should rot in there." She stuck to her story of not knowing LaFontaine when the Spanish-speaking investigator spoke to her a second time in October. The week before, Gerry Belliveau had interviewed Dolores's former upstairs neighbor, a cop named Hector, who had seen LaFontaine and Dolores together in her apartment on one occasion after she had left her husband. But when confronted with Hector's story, Dolores insisted again that she did not know LaFontaine and repeated what she had said about Carlos at the first interview: "I hope he rots in jail."

Carlos was sure that Dolores knew LaFontaine even before the officer arrested him. Not long after they first met, Dolores had asked him whether he knew LaFontaine. When he answered no, she said, "He was the one who arrested you." Carlos had not mentioned his arrest, but she knew about it, she said, because one of the men who lived in her building was a friend of LaFontaine, and he was often in the house. "Pay attention," she warned Carlos, "because he is a bad guy." But Carlos didn't pay attention because he knew he was innocent. Cocky, naive, and stubborn, he ignored all the signs of trouble.

After Mike Keating interviewed Carlos about Dolores, he said to me, "It sounds like that house where she lived was filled with cops and Carlos got in the way." (Belliveau had the same impression.) Mike also thought that Carlos's innocence had worked against him, making him believe no harm would come to him. "He reminds me of Billy Budd," Mike said.

In mid-November our New York investigator interviewed Dolores's ex-husband, "Marco," in New Jersey. When the investigator showed Marco a picture of LaFontaine, he recognized him as the officer who was with Dolores on the day Marco appeared in court for kidnapping his son. Marco and his relatives had thought it was odd that LaFontaine stayed in court almost all day with Dolores.

Now we knew that almost certainly Dolores lied about knowing LaFontaine. Not only had she been seen with the officer in court, by both Carlos and her ex-husband, and in her apartment by Hector, but she had told Carlos about him. What was her motive now for denying she knew him? Was it the vindictiveness of a scorned woman?

With Dolores stonewalling, we could not prove that LaFontaine had a motive to frame Carlos. All we could show was that at the time LaFontaine testified against Carlos, he had an undisclosed bias against him. Would that be enough to help in our uphill battle?

In late November Carlos was put into solitary confinement — the hole. A rapist had been beaten up in his dormitory, and they punished everyone, Evelin told me. The authorities held a trial inside the prison and told Carlos to plead guilty. He refused, saying, "I went through this on the outside. I'm not going through it again." A rat ran over his head while he was sleeping. "What else do I have to go through?" he lamented to Evelin. He stuffed toilet paper in the holes to keep the rats away.

After he got out of the hole, he wrote a Christmas card to me, with these words:

> I am cain of sad for my situation, but with your help and counting on God and all of you, I hope that I can be home for the next Christmas and not here in this place.

I held little Carlos in my arms and paced slowly back and forth in the children's area of the prison visitors' room. Although almost two now, little Carlos seemed light as a doll. He weighed less than his baby brother, Neftalee, not yet a year old, who was born after Carlos went to prison. Neftalee, who looked like a miniature Japanese wrestler, was being carried by Carlos's inmate friend Felix, also pacing in the children's room. Josua was there too, playing on the floor. Felix and I were minding the children while Evelin translated for Carlos the motion that I had brought with me in a manila folder.

Through the glass wall I could see the two of them sitting at the far end of the visitors' room: their heads together, their eyes fixed on the typewritten sheet that Evelin held up, following the text with her finger as she translated. Both of them looked utterly absorbed in the words that could win Carlos his freedom.

The day before — Saturday, December 9 — Mike had come into the bookstore with the final version for me to deliver to Carlos. He should sign both copies of the motion, Mike instructed. Later, they would send him a copy of the whole package, including the brief that Gary was preparing — a memorandum in support of the motion — an affidavit from Belliveau, and Pablo Osario's affidavit. Mike was hopeful that everything would be ready to file in the next week.

It took a long time for Evelin to translate the nine-page motion, but the little boy in my arms did not fuss. He seemed mesmerized by a card that he had plucked off a shelf. Like the wall-size mural in the room, the card depicted Snow White and the Seven Dwarfs. Little Carlos held it reverently, touching the figures one by one with his tiny index finger. He was so absorbed in the picture that he did not seem to notice the kisses that I planted on his head.

At a sign from Evelin that they were done, I joined them at their seats, letting little Carlos down to play with Josua. We had been allowed to bring in the legal documents but not a pen, and Carlos walked to the guard's table to borrow one. As he sat down again, he exaggerated the shaking of his hand, and we all laughed. Using his knees as a desk, he signed both copies, and I carefully returned them to the manila folder.

With Orange Crush again from the vending machine, we drank a toast. Evelin raised her plastic cup: "To coming home."

"To justice," I added.

The three of us touched our cups together for a long, sweet

moment, beaming at each other. And then we drank: To coming home. To justice.

A few days later Carlos began receiving the cards I had asked people to send when it became clear that he would be spending another Christmas in prison. The first that arrived came from my mother in Oklahoma. Then two or three a day, more than twenty in all. Carlos's fellow inmates were amazed: "You must have lots of friends." Some of the cards were from out of state — my friend Danny in California sent one with an added message from his Hispanic maid — but most came from my own neighborhood. The guards who delivered the mail must have wondered why Carlos was Beacon Hill's favorite inmate.

The motion for a new trial was filed while I was away in Tulsa celebrating Christmas with my family. On New Year's Day, Mike put a copy of the final document through my mail slot. A friend visiting from Scotland read the whole thing — motion, memorandum, and affidavits — and then said, "They have to let him go. No rational person could do anything else." Coming from an interested but objective source, his words heartened me, and I too felt that the document was eloquent and powerful. But the only opinion that really mattered was that of Judge Elizabeth Porada.

"We're over the first hurdle," Mike told me when word finally came in late January. In response to the motion for a new trial, Judge Porada asked for an evidentiary hearing and agreed to our request for a copy of the transcript from the second trial, to be paid for by the state. She instructed Mike Keating and Gary Crossen to get in touch with Lynn Beland to schedule a hearing at the earliest possible date. "We were afraid we wouldn't get this far," Mike admitted.

When Gary spoke to Beland, he told her, "Give some thought as to whether we can settle this amicably and quietly. If you think there are merits to our case, we can avoid the need for an evidentiary hearing. He's been in prison for nearly eighteen months — you've got your pound of flesh. And you're not going to retry him; you haven't got a witness." Beland was defensive and not inclined to go along with us, but she acknowledged that others in the D.A.'s office might feel differently. She did not reject the idea out of hand.

About a week after the word from Porada, Ed DeMore called me one morning at the bookstore. "I was talking to Mike the other night, and I was wondering if you realize how optimistic he is."

"I know he's more optimistic than Gary." In his usual skeptic's role, Gary had cautioned me that the odds were still on the prosecution's side.

"Well, he's very optimistic. He says if there's a hearing, LaFontaine will take the Fifth because of his other case. Mike's only concern is getting it done before Judge Porada moves up to the Appeals Court." The hearing, if the D.A.'s office did not agree to forego it, would mean two days in Springfield, in western Massachusetts, where Porada was now sitting. "That's a big investment for Mike's firm," Ed told me. Foley, Hoag was continuing to represent Carlos without charge.

The lawyers were working for free, but the private detectives had to be paid; Ed and I were both raising money to cover the mounting costs. Many of the donors had also sent Christmas cards to Carlos. He was overwhelmed when he received them and wrote me a letter at the end of January.

Dear Linda:

I hope and wish that you and your family are alright and I want you to know that I wish you all the best on this New Year. Linda, I feel so happy because I know that all you people care for me and your friends too on my situation. I don't know how can I pay you all you have done for me, but I'm so thankfull...

Listen: this is true: I have never in my all life have recieve so beautiful cards as the ones I got from you and so beautiful poems like the ones that you and your friends send me for Christmas. I want you to thank each one of them for me.

Linda, I feel so happy that is difficult for me to find words to thank you, but I have faith in God and you that am going to live this place because this place is not for me and I'm inocent of all this. But God has put you in my life to make a chance. I will always keep you in my heart and all my thoughts...

Yours truelly, Carlos Montilla

By mid-February it was clear that the D.A.'s office was not going to let the case go. The evidentiary hearing was scheduled for March 1 at the Suffolk County Courthouse in Boston, not in Springfield after all. That was wonderful news, making it much easier for everyone — lawyers, witnesses, and spectators like me.

"We're on top of it," Gary assured me two days before the hearing. The previous day they had finally received the transcript of LaFontaine's testimony at the second trial. Both he and Mike read it overnight and discussed it at breakfast that morning, dividing the witnesses and gearing up.

"Did you get LaFontaine?"

"Yes, but he's frustrating to gear up for. I can't imagine he's going to testify."

"Maybe he'll get on the stand and say he made a mistake."

"Fat chance!" Gary scoffed.

I asked, "Did Mike tell you what Carlos said about you two?"

"No, he didn't."

"Carlos is so happy —"

"I hope he's not getting his hopes too high," Gary interjected.

"No, no, he isn't; he's very nervous. But he's very happy you and Mike are going into court for him. He says, 'Mike looks so nice and noble, just by his face, he'll convince anyone. And the way Gary talks he'll convince anyone.'"

"Wait until he hears me yell and scream," Gary said. I could tell by his voice that he was smiling.

The day before the hearing was Ash Wednesday. I had not been to church for several months but planned to go that evening. "I'm going to say a prayer today anyway and maybe it would be better in church," I told Evelin when we spoke that morning.

She had the same thought. "I haven't been to church since Josua was a baby. But Carlos goes every other day in prison."

Carlos did not want her to see him in chains, she said. "Last time when he went into court on the appeal Warren laughed at him."

"No one is going to laugh at him this time," I assured her.

That evening at the Church of the Advent's Solemn Mass, after imposition of the ashes and communion, I knelt to say a prayer for Carlos, finishing with "Thy will be done." That was the proper end to a prayer, I believed. Except for those moments of crisis when you can't help yourself, you shouldn't go begging to God. But as sometimes happened at the end of my daily prayers, the words in my heart came involuntarily to my lips: "Please let him come home." And with those words, as always, came tears I could not stop. *Please let him come home.*

seventeen

A FEW MINUTES AFTER TEN o'clock, Judge Elizabeth Porada emerged from her chambers and spoke to the court officer. He picked up the phone on the courtroom wall and called the holding tank where Carlos was waiting. "I've got Judge Porada here champing at the bit," he said.

A middle-aged woman with short auburn hair, Porada wore large glasses that gave her an owlish, professorial look. A white, ascoted blouse filled in the V-neck of her black robe. Her narrow, intelligent face had a no-nonsense expression, an expression that said, "I do not suffer fools gladly and let's get on with this."

In her impatience would the judge notice the variety of people gathered here for Carlos, the young man whose fate was in her hands?

We were on the ninth floor of the Suffolk County Courthouse, in courtroom 916, the same room where Carlos was tried the second time, before this same judge, and convicted. A mirror image of the courtroom for the first trial — with the jury box to the left of the judge's bench instead of the right

— it had the same oak paneling to the ceiling, the same tall, grimy windows on two sides, the same scuffed and dingy look.

I sat in the front row of the oak pews for spectators with my friend Mary from New Hampshire, who had followed the story from the beginning and been a generous donor, and Claudia, the young Columbian woman who had visited the prison twice with Mike Keating as a volunteer translator. Close by was my Beacon Hill neighbor Mrs. Eacker, the elegant older woman who had given me, unsolicited, the first donation to help Carlos. Rachel, Gary's secretary, had come too, not wanting to miss this act of the drama.

Behind us were Evelin and her contingent: four adults and her son Josua, who had begged to come. Wearing a blue jacket and a tie, he sat with his short legs dangling over the edge of the seat. He was squirming with excitement. I turned around to smile at him, and he grinned, showing front teeth that were too large for his small, rather exotic face, a typical young boy's smile. But this eight-year-old had just made a valentine for the only father he had ever known, a valentine that showed a man behind bars inside a large heart.

More players sat in the short side rows: Hector, Dolores's former upstairs neighbor, wearing his police uniform; a tall young man from the police department holding a thick file folder: LaFontaine's internal affairs record, subpoenaed by Mike and Gary; Officer Edward Fleming, also in uniform, whom I had seen earlier in the hall and instantly recognized — his barrel chest and lumbering walk were unmistakable. But no LaFontaine.

As we waited, Gerry Belliveau arrived and sat down with a tall, dark-haired man wearing a green workman's jumpsuit and tortoise-shell glasses. He slouched forward with his elbows on his knees, his expression defiant and uncomfortable. This was our star witness, Pablo Osario.

"I pulled him out of the sixth floor of the warehouse where he works," Belliveau whispered to me. "He's not very happy."

A side door opened and Carlos, his hands cuffed in front of him, walked in, escorted by a guard. He was wearing his wedding clothes — the white brocade shirt and black tuxedo pants, but no jacket. Behind me I heard Josua exclaim, "Poppy!" Carlos scanned the spectators and smiled, his dark eyes shining. He took his place at the defendant's table next to Mike, who draped his arm around Carlos's shoulders; the two men talked with their heads close together. Gary was on the other side of Mike, at the left end of the wooden table; the interpreter, a man with a ponytail, sat next to Carlos on the other end.

Lynn Beland and another assistant D.A., a tall man who had helped her carry in stacks of file folders, stood talking at the prosecutor's table in front of the clerk's corral. She looked sour and annoyed.

"All rise," the clerk called out, and Judge Porada entered and took the bench. Counsel identified themselves, and Mike and then Gary stood up for Carlos: not one, but two corporate attorneys in court for the indigent young prisoner.

Mike, in his opening statement, reviewed the four new facts that were not available at Montilla's trial: First, LaFontaine's testimony about the physical layout of the scene and the apartment window had been shown not to be credible. Second, Pablo Osario, now available as a witness, said he did not know Montilla and told a similar story about LaFontaine taking his license from his wallet. Third, the relationship between Carlos, LaFontaine, and Dolores had not been revealed. Finally,

LaFontaine's current problems and the revelations about his police record discredited the sole identifying witness. "We believe these factors directly relate to this man's innocence," Mike said.

Beland, when it was her turn, sounded like someone greatly aggrieved. Her tone seemed to say, Why are we wasting time on this ridiculous matter? No newly discovered evidence had been presented, she said. The scene was available to the jurors, and they had viewed the hallway. LaFontaine's subsequent problems were irrelevant, she said. "They are totally separate and unrelated matters." As for his police record, a motion to subpoena his file had been presented to Porada prior to trial, but the motion was denied. "The Commonwealth's position to the court is going to be that none of this is newly discovered," Beland finished, without saying a word about Pablo Osario.

Judge Porada leaned forward, her hands cupped in front of her. "I will be very frank with both of you. I gave you a hearing, Mr. Keating, for two reasons. One was the fact that we now have Mr. Osario, who we did not have at the time of the trial. And two, there have been allegations of extortion — simply allegations at this particular time — of alleged drug suspects by the sole identifying and sole material witness at the trial."

She cocked her head skeptically and spoke directly to Mike. "With respect to the view, I remember going out on the view, quite frankly. While the apartment was under renovation, still we could have climbed the stairs if the defense counsel had elected. So the location as such, and what you could see and what you could not see, and the window — which you also brought out and I find interesting — may affect whether justice was done or not at the trial. But I may say that those avenues were open to defense counsel at Mr. Montilla's earlier trial.

At least that is my thinking at this time. I am being very frank and candid."

Mike stood up to say, "I appreciate your candor. Could I make a ten-second response? I think it's material to your comment, Your Honor." Mike explained his understanding of the case law in the Commonwealth: evidence that was discoverable at the time could be considered in a motion for a new trial if it was presented along with new evidence that could not have been discovered with reasonable diligence.

"I don't disagree with your assessment of the law," Porada said, smiling slightly.

Gary Crossen and Lynn Beland then argued about LaFontaine's internal affairs record being turned over, and after listening to both sides, Judge Porada ordered the documents produced.

"Your Honor, the whole file?" Beland asked, clearly dismayed.

"I would allow the order limited to any allegations involving drug investigations or drug arrests," the judge answered. "I think for purposes of discovery the defense counsel is entitled to at least look at that internal investigation file, and I'm going to order them produced."

Beland asked for some time, and the judge ordered a five-minute recess. Carlos was taken out of the courtroom, and a few moments later, someone came to fetch Evelin, and they stood talking just outside the metal side door. Pablo, looking more relaxed now, was sitting next to Mrs. Eacker, who chatted him up as well as she could with his limited English. The two of them made an odd pair, the Beacon Hill matron and the young Hispanic in workman's clothes. I introduced myself to Pablo, explaining, "I've been working to help Carlos."

He nodded and said, "Yes, I want to help him too."

Beland and the other assistant D.A. were still going through LaFontaine's file when Judge Porada returned and stood at the bench. "I understand there's a disagreement as to what records should be produced," she said impatiently.

"Actually, Your Honor, it is more a clarification," Beland responded. She was not certain exactly what reports to turn over.

"I think the simplest thing is to turn it all over. I will order that you produce the entire file."

At our seats, Mary and I turned to each other and smiled. "She took too long," Mary whispered. "She outfoxed herself."

"If you would call your first witness," Porada said to Mike.

When Carlos took the stand, the judge swiveled her tall-backed leather chair to look directly at him. She rested her temple on her hand and studied him intently throughout his testimony. She was hearing him speak for the first time.

Through the interpreter, Mike asked Carlos the questions they had prepared. Carlos answered calmly, with no sign of the nervousness he showed at the first trial. A ray of sunshine slanted through the tall window behind him and lit up his left shoulder, the one closest to the judge.

Mike asked if he had ever in his life been arrested before the night of the incident, and Carlos answered, "No."

"Prior to the convictions under the sentence that you're serving now, have you ever been convicted of a crime before?"

"No."

He was twenty-five, Carlos stated, born in Santo Domingo, Dominican Republic; he had come to the United States seven years ago; he had a ninth-grade education. At the time of his arrest, he lived in Roxbury.

"Were you employed?"

"I worked in various places. I was working in a factory...a company that made car brakes." (Would Beland catch him in this inconsistency with his prior testimony, when he said he was laid off at the time of his arrest?)

"Are you married?"

"Yes, I'm married."

"Where were you married?"

"In the prison."

"Do you have children?"

"Two children."

"How old are your children?"

"One is two years old. One is one year old. And then there is an eight-year-old that I brought up."

The next questions were about "Dolores" and Carlos's romantic relationship with her. He met her in the autumn before his arrest, he said. They lived together for ten to twelve days around Christmas and the New Year, and the relationship ended when he left in January.

"Did she protest your leaving?"

"Yes. She protested."

"What did she do?"

"She got very furious, and she called me very bad names. She called me an asshole and a bastard and that I would pay for everything that I had done."

Mike asked when Carlos next saw Dolores, and he answered, "In the court." It was just a few days after he had left her. She was with LaFontaine, the officer who had arrested him, and Edward Fleming, the officer who took him from the Catania Club that night. Mike asked if Dolores had said anything to him, and Carlos answered yes. She told him he was going to spend three years in prison. (But Carlos did not mention that Dolores had laughed and laughed.)

Yes, Dolores knew that he had been arrested even though he never told her about it. "I don't know how she knew, but she knew it, because she asked me." Yes, she told Carlos she was friendly with police officers, including Hector, her upstairs neighbor. "She told me that all of her relations or her friendships are with police."

Mike, talking directly to the translator, asked if he could remember whether Dolores said anything else to him during that conversation about his arrest. "Well, yes, she told me that I should be careful." (Carlos forgot to say that Dolores warned him LaFontaine was "a bad guy.") No, he had never seen Dolores again after that day in court.

Mike then asked if Carlos ever said anything to Albert LaFontaine about Dolores. "Yes.... I don't remember the exact day, but it was here outside of the courtroom on the ninth floor just before that trial was beginning." Carlos had said to LaFontaine, "I know why you are doing all of this to me" — because of Dolores. "He told me I was inventing this, why was I inventing this."

Mike, addressing Carlos as "Mr. Montilla," asked him what he was doing on the night he was arrested. Now the judge would hear Carlos's version for the first time.

"Well, I was in a club that I'm a member of playing pool and drinking a couple of beers." Yes, he was outside the club when he was arrested, and yes, he remembered being approached by a police officer. No, he had not been anywhere near the Geneva project or 223 Geneva Avenue that night or any other time. "I've never visited that place."

Did he know why the police took him to the police station? "They told me that I was arrested for drinking a beer in the street, for drinking in public, that's why they arrested me."

Yes, he had turned over his personal property to the police at the station, and yes, that included his wallet with the pay stub inside. The wallet was returned to him, but not the pay stub.

Mike then asked if Carlos knew Pablo Osario, and he answered, "No, I don't know him." Pablo was asked to rise and stood with his hands clasped in front of him.

"Until this morning, have you ever seen that man before in your life?"

Carlos shook his head. "*Nunca.*" Never.

It was Lynn Beland's turn. Unlike Mike, who had stood up at his seat, Beland walked to the microphone at the end of the empty jury box to ask her questions. She began right away with Dolores, confirming the period when she and Carlos had been together. "And during that time I think you just told Your Honor you were living with her, right?"

"Yes, I was living with her."

Beland asked if he remembered testifying under oath at his first trial, and Carlos answered yes. As Beland asked about his prior testimony, when he said he was living with Evelin, Mike flipped through his copy of the first trial transcript and then looked over at the prosecutor. "Could I have a page on that?" he asked.

"I don't have a page."

"Well, I mean, are you quoting from the transcript or not?" Mike persisted.

"No, I'm not," Beland snapped. "I'm asking a question, if that's acceptable." She then repeated her question to Carlos about the contradiction in his testimony.

"Your Honor, I object," Mike said. "I don't think it's inconsistent. He said he lived for twelve days with the other woman in a period between October and January."

Beland rolled her eyes and said, "I have no other questions," returning to her seat.

In redirect, Mike asked Carlos, "Did LaFontaine ever say to you at any time that you should leave the United States?"

"Twice he said that to me."

"Do you recall what he said to you on either of those occasions?"

"Yes, I remember. He told me that there was still time for me to go, yes, to my country."

"Did you reply to him?"

"Yes. I told him I wasn't going anywhere because I hadn't done anything."

Mike was now finished, but Judge Porada had questions of her own. She asked Carlos if he knew Dolores at the time of his arrest in October, and Carlos replied, "Yes, I knew her."

"You had no relationship with her until December?"

"Well, as far as the relationship, we talked to each other. She said to me that she was hoping to divorce her husband and — so, yeah, I knew her." (With his wife in the courtroom, what else could Carlos say?)

"You may step down, Mr. Montilla."

Gary then called Gerry Belliveau to the stand and established that Belliveau had worked as a Secret Service agent for fifteen years and as a private investigator since then; that he was retained a year ago to work on the Montilla case; and that the previous April he had visited the scene of the alleged crime at 223 Geneva Avenue. Approaching the witness stand, Gary showed Belliveau five photographs taken during that visit. These photographs, after being identified, were marked and admitted as Exhibits 1 through 5. They showed both the rear of the building and interior shots, including a close-up of the kitchen window.

"What did you observe, sir, with respect to the kitchen window in Apartment 3E as to how it opened and closed?"

"Rather than opening and closing up and down as testified to by Officer LaFontaine, the windows opened from side to side. They slid from side to side." Belliveau also determined from his investigation that the windows had not been changed since the time of the alleged crime. He observed the kitchen window from the outside and estimated it was approximately twenty-five feet from the ground and about four feet from the roof.

Gary asked Belliveau if, in his opinion, someone could jump from the window without injuring himself.

"One could jump, but one would probably injure himself."

"Did you make a determination, sir, as to whether it was possible for someone to vault to the roof from the sliding sideways window?"

"Well, there is no ledge there. I suppose it would be possible. But again it would be very difficult."

Gary then established that the adjacent master bedroom window was the only other rear exit from Apartment 3E beyond the kitchen window and the kitchen door. The bedroom window was like the one in the kitchen, sliding from side to side and in the same position relative to the roof and the ground.

"Now, sir, did you examine as well the front stairwell for Apartment 3E?"

"Yes, I did." And yes, he was familiar with LaFontaine's testimony. No, it was not possible at any point between the second and third floors to see through the stairs and observe Apartment 3E.

"If you positioned yourself halfway between the second and third floors, do you know how far away from Apartment 3E's front door you would be?"

"Approximately ten feet."

"Do you know, sir, whether you would be easily observable from Apartment 3E's front door?"

"Yes, you would be."

"Do you know if there is any location to hide in that area?"

"No, there isn't."

"Do you know, sir, how wide the stairwell is going from the second floor to the third floor?"

"Approximately three feet."

Gary then brought Belliveau's attention to Exhibit 5, showing two males standing in front of a door, and Exhibit 2, showing the door with no one in front of it. "Sir, how much space is there outside the door at unit 3E?"

"On the landing area? Approximately five to six feet."

"In your experience, sir, is it possible for an individual to have gone up those stairs and hit, physically hit that door; that is, put his shoulder to the door, while three people are standing in front of that door without hitting those people?"

Beland's objection was sustained, and I made a mental note to ask Gary why he put the question that way. At the first trial, LaFontaine testified that the black males had already run down the stairs when he put his shoulder to the door.

Gary asked Belliveau if there was any point on the stairwell where one could look through the stairs and see the front door of Apartment 3E, and Belliveau answered, "Not through the stairs, no."

The next witness would have been Pablo, but his lawyer was not yet in court; because of the potential for self-incrimination, Pablo could not testify without him. Instead Hector was called to the stand, and Mike and then Beland questioned him. He testified that he was a Boston police officer and had known LaFontaine as a fellow officer for fifteen years. He also knew Dolores and her former husband, who had lived on the second floor of the building where Hector and his wife lived in the third-floor apartment. LaFontaine visited Hector's apartment on one occasion, he said, staying less than an hour. That same winter day, Hector saw LaFontaine with Dolores in her apartment; her husband was not there. It was his understanding that LaFontaine was there "for her safety," to protect her while she collected some belongings. (She had left her husband a month or so before.) That was the only time he saw LaFontaine in her apartment. Hector was then excused.

Neither LaFontaine nor Dolores was yet in court, despite being subpoenaed. If they did not appear, Gary told the judge, they would ask her to issue warrants to arrest them. Porada said she would only do that if she had proof they had been served in hand. "You will have that immediately," Gary answered, promising to bring in David Prum, the person from Belliveau's office who had served the subpoenas. Pablo's attorney, Arnold Abelow, was still not in court. Porada, who had two other hearings scheduled for that day and wanted to proceed as quickly as possible, ordered a five-minute recess. "You find out why Mr. Abelow is not present," she said.

Toward the end of the recess Mike and Gary returned to the defense table, and I walked over to talk with them. The transcript from the second trial, highlighted with yellow, lay open on the table. I asked Gary about the way he framed the question to Belliveau about LaFontaine and the door. "At the first trial LaFontaine told us he tried to break down the door *after* the three males ran down the stairs."

"Well, at the second trial, he testified they were still in front of the door when he put his shoulder to it," Gary explained.

I shook my head. "That's ridiculous. How could anyone believe that?" LaFontaine had told an even more implausible story at the second trial, yet twelve people had bought it.

When Porada returned to the courtroom, Mike and Gary told her that they were still unable to reach Pablo's attorney and asked for a recess until later in the afternoon. The judge agreed to take an early recess for lunch until 1:15, when she would hear David Prum testify and decide whether to issue bench warrants for LaFontaine and Dolores. Except for Prum's testimony, our case was recessed until 2:30, although she could not guarantee it would go forward then.

At the lunch break, the Carlos contingent split up. My neighbor Mrs. Eacker, my friend Mary, and Gary's secretary, Rachel, left for the day, regretfully unable to stay longer. Gerry Belliveau took Pablo out to eat; Evelin and her group went off together; Claudia, the volunteer translator, did something on her own. I ate lunch with Mike and Gary at a cafeteria across the plaza from the courthouse. The lawyers' trays looked like they were carbo-loading for a marathon, but I had only a bowl of soup.

Gary had brought with him LaFontaine's police file and read it through between bites, making notes on his legal pad. When he took a break from it, I asked him a question that had occurred to me that morning: "Does the D.A.'s office have a blacklist for jurors?"

"Yes," Gary deadpanned, "but there's only one name on it."

I laughed and said, "Who could that be?"

Lunch over, we walked back across the plaza and into the courthouse, where my mood again turned apprehensive. What would the afternoon bring? Would Pablo be able to take the stand? And, of course, the most disturbing question mark of all: LaFontaine.

eighteen

SHORTLY AFTER THREE O'CLOCK A small, balding man stepped off the elevator, unbuttoning his camel's-hair jacket, eyes cast down. Preoccupied, I barely glanced at him. When I finished pacing the length of the hall and returned to Gary and Evelin at other end, she pointed in the man's direction and said, "Did you see him?"

"Who?" I said.

"LaFontaine. Don't you recognize him since his lawyer cleaned up his act?" Gary teased.

I was dumbfounded. "I don't believe it — he walked right past me. Where is he now?" I asked Evelin.

"Around the corner. He's hiding."

Even though I had not recognized him, now that I knew he was here — that he had walked right past me — butterflies began to dance in my stomach, a slow waltz, nothing like the fandango that came later.

Willie Davis, LaFontaine's lawyer, had appeared in court after lunch. A good-looking black man, heavyset and well dressed, Davis often represented accused officers; his name frequently appeared in the newspapers. He told the judge that LaFontaine was not deliberately not honoring the subpoena, which had indeed been served in hand (as Dolores's had not). He was waiting, Davis said, to find out if he had to appear. Because of his current status — under indictment and awaiting trial — LaFontaine would invoke the Fifth on all questions except his name and address; he would not even admit he was a police officer. Nevertheless, Judge Porada told Davis to have LaFontaine in court at three o'clock.

It was after three now, but the hearing before ours was still going on. We who were waiting milled around in the hall, both idle and alert, like passengers listening for a boarding call. Groups formed, dissolved, re-formed. Pablo, agitated and restless, paced back and forth outside the courtroom while Belliveau sat stoically on one of the benches. Approaching Pablo with a sympathetic smile, I asked, "How are you doing?"

"This waiting, it drives me crazy."

"I know, me too. But it's very important for you to be here. You can make all the difference for Carlos. We are very grateful to you."

His face softened, and we chatted for a while, then he resumed his pacing, swinging his arms and slapping his hands together, fist against palm. I was worried about his taking the stand when he was so worked up. I sat down next to Belliveau and said, "Pablo acts like he's about to explode."

The detective grimaced. "It's been a long day."

"It's a good thing you're here to keep an eye on him," I said.

"Pablo's lawyer is still not here," Belliveau said, "but I understand LaFontaine has arrived."

"Yes, I know. He's keeping himself out of sight around the corner."

After a few moments' silence, Belliveau said, "It makes you wonder, what happens to a guy like LaFontaine. He started out as a good cop."

"I find that really hard to believe."

"No, it's true," Belliveau said. "A very good cop."

It was four o'clock before we were called back to the courtroom. The long middle rows still had people in them, so I sat down in the first of the two side benches on the right. With my coat piled next to me, there was no room left on the seat. I opened my yellow legal pad to resume taking notes. Behind me the courtroom door opened, and I turned my head to look.

Now I recognized him — the grooved face, the deep-set eyes, the pale moustache. Our eyes met briefly — mine widened in alarm but no flicker from him — did he know who I was? He sat down right behind me. LaFontaine.

A second or so later, Belliveau entered and sat down next to LaFontaine, giving me a reassuring nod that did not stop the pounding of my heart. Next, Fleming, who stood behind LaFontaine and bent down to whisper in his ear — what was he saying? — and then came forward to the bench where I was sitting, unceremoniously lifting up my coat to make room for himself. I took the coat and deposited it on the floor by my feet.

With a shaky hand I began to write on the yellow pad, holding it at an angle so Fleming could not see the words. Maybe he'd think I was a reporter. I knew Fleming must have recognized Belliveau from his appearance on the stand that morning, but would he know who I was?

Judge Porada began, "We have a few housekeeping matters, I think, first of all. One is the presence of Mr. LaFontaine. Is he here?"

Gary answered, "He is." (Yes, he is here, sitting behind me. I cannot see him without turning my shoulders, but I feel him there, my back prickling.)

"He is here with counsel?"

"Yes, Your Honor."

"Also, Mr. Osario?"

"Without counsel. We tried all afternoon to reach his lawyer who we understood was going to be here today."

"Well, I don't think Mr. Osario can testify in this matter without the presence of his counsel," Porada said to Gary.

"The defendant then would call Al LaFontaine to the stand."

I watched him walk past me, saw his profile — the prominent nose and small chin — then his back. There was no trace of the arrogant swagger I remembered from the trial. He swore to tell the truth and took his seat in the witness chair. Davis sat near him, at the end of the jury box closest to the stand.

At the defendant's table, Gary stood in his characteristic posture, hands on hips, index fingers hooked over his belt, and began his questions. LaFontaine gave his name and home address. Gary then asked, "Your occupation?"

LaFontaine read haltingly from a slip of paper in his hand: "On the advice of counsel, I decline to answer and assert my privilege under the Fifth Amendment of the Constitution of the United States." For some reason he emphasized the word *under*; otherwise his voice was toneless.

"Until recently, Mr. LaFontaine, were you an officer of the Boston Police Department?"

"On the advice of my counsel, I decline to answer and assert my privilege *under* the Fifth Amendment of the Constitution of the United States."

Bent head, halting voice — this was not the man I had seen on the stand almost two years before. Gone was the smirk, the self-satisfied grin, the undisguised contempt for the defense attorney. This was a diminished man, reciting from a slip of paper his privilege not to incriminate himself.

"Sir, have you ever been subject to internal Boston Police Department discipline for providing false information to departmental inquiries?"

"On advice of my counsel, I decline to answer...."

Question after question got the same answer. Porada listened with her chin on her hand, scrutinizing LaFontaine. Finally, Gary said to her, "Your Honor, I'd like the record to reflect that I have many, many questions that I would pose to Officer LaFontaine. But I think the record is quite clear that he will continue to invoke the Fifth Amendment. It seems to me it's not in anyone's best interest to continue." Gary then asked Porada to consider compelling LaFontaine to answer questions about his relationship with Dolores and about the conversations with Mr. Montilla.

Porada, as usual, listened with an appraising look on her face and then ruled that LaFontaine's answers might lead to incriminating statements or possible criminal prosecutions. "So I am not going to compel him to answer those questions," she said, raising her hand for emphasis. She then asked Beland if she had any questions of this witness, and the prosecutor answered no.

LaFontaine walked away from the stand, eyes down, fingers fiddling with his coat buttons. As he passed the bench where I was sitting, Fleming stood and followed him out. He was gone, and except for newspaper photographs, I never saw him again, except now and then in a bad dream.

Pablo's attorney was still not in court. "I wish we could reach Mr. Abelow," Judge Porada said, "because I could be back tomorrow. I would just as soon wrap this up if I could." Both Mike and Gary left the courtroom to try again.

I moved over to the middle section to sit next to Evelin, now by herself except for Josua. Everyone else, my friends too, had left at lunchtime, unable to stay longer. The lawyers returned shortly to report still no luck on Abelow, but Mike had found out his home number, and they hoped to reach him that evening.

"All right," Porada said. "I am willing to take a chance and put this on tentatively for tomorrow." After Porada confirmed with the court reporter that she could be present at nine o'clock the next morning, the young woman who was Carlos's afternoon interpreter volunteered, "I can be here also." "Me, too," the court officer said. Maybe it was wishful thinking on my part, but I sensed that they both had more than a professional interest, that they were rooting for Carlos.

"One small point, Your Honor," Mike said. He now had the complete trial transcript and wondered if she would like to see a copy before tomorrow. "I have no objection to having my memory refreshed by looking at it," she answered, with the slight, sardonic smile that we had seen several times that day.

I turned to Evelin and whispered, "Good. She can't miss all of LaFontaine's lies."

As Carlos was led from the courtroom, he turned to smile at Evelin and me, and I gave him a thumbs-up sign. Mike came over to talk to us. "There's no chance it will be settled tomorrow," he cautioned. "The best we can hope for is that she will take it under advisement. And she could dismiss it out of hand, but I doubt she'll do that."

He and Evelin and I stood talking while Gary, coat on and briefcase in hand, waited in the aisle, listening. Josua sat huddled, silent and alone, in the corner of the pew. Then he began to cry, tears running down his face. "I thought Daddy was coming home today. I want him to come home. I don't like to see him in handcuffs." And then he repeated, "I thought he was coming home today."

It was Gary who went to him, kneeling down to put his arm around the heartbroken little boy. "We're working on it," he said. "Be patient."

I'll never forget that image: Gary in his overcoat, kneeling down with his briefcase in one hand, the other arm around Josua's shoulders — the warm comfort of the gesture and the cool reality of a lawyer's words: "We're working on it. Be patient." I watched in silence, too moved to say anything.

The next morning Evelin told me that Josua had cried all night. He kept saying, "I want Daddy to come home. I don't like to see him in handcuffs." She looked close to tears herself. "I shouldn't have brought him," she said, "but he begged me so hard."

By nine o'clock a reduced cast had gathered: Evelin, me, Belliveau, Mike, Gary, and Pablo's lawyer, Arnold Abelow, who was waiting inside the courtroom. But no Pablo.

"Where's Pablo?" I asked Belliveau, assuming he had brought him again.

"He's driving in on his own today," Belliveau said, and when he saw the alarm on my face, quickly added, "Pablo promised me he'd be here."

What if he didn't show up after all this? I looked at my watch: 9:05. We would be called into the courtroom any minute.

I could feel my nerves tighten and tingle, something close to panic sweeping over me. Evelin, who had been pacing, walked over to me and asked, "Where's Pablo?" When I told her he was coming on his own, she too was alarmed. An elevator bell dinged, and we both turned to look. The door opened, the person who stepped out was not Pablo. A few seconds later another ding and several people got off. None was Pablo. I sat down next to Mike on one of the benches. He was reading a law book, seemingly unperturbed by Pablo's absence. An elevator dinged again, more people, no Pablo.

Ten minutes and several elevator loads later, I was convinced Pablo would not show up. He's not coming, I thought in despair. Why should he? There's nothing in it for him. I did not even look up at the sound of another elevator bell until I heard Mike say, "That's him." And Pablo stepped off the elevator.

I jumped up and held out my arms as though he were the prodigal son: "Pablo!" For a second he looked taken aback, and then he beamed. I shook his hand, and then Mike shook his hand, saying, "I like your jacket." It was a silky black bomber jacket with a decorative name on the sleeve; underneath it he wore a gray sweatshirt and gray slacks. He was much more presentable than the day before.

Evelin, returning from the water fountain, gave Pablo a big smile: "You're here!" He grinned, looking like a man who unexpectedly finds himself carried on the shoulders of a cheering crowd. I doubt that he will ever be so warmly greeted again as that morning when he came in on his own to help Carlos.

Before going into the courtroom, Mike and Gary and Pablo's lawyer huddled in the foyer with Pablo and the interpreter. They were making sure he understood his rights not to incriminate himself. Pablo had gotten there in good time after all; it was 9:30 before we began. "Good morning," Judge Porada said from the bench. "Mr. Osario is now present?"

"Yes, Your Honor, he is. His attorney, Mr. Abelow, is here as well," Gary said. "They have spoken. I think we are prepared to go forward."

Judge Porada addressed Pablo herself, to make sure he understood he was waiving his right not to incriminate himself. "After talking to your lawyer and after hearing what I have just told you, do you still want to testify at this hearing?"

Pablo answered yes, and after swearing to tell the truth, he sat down in the witness chair, already looking nervous. He was now in gray from head to foot, having shed his black jacket. In answer to Gary's questions, Pablo testified that he had lived in Brockton for three years and worked at his job there for two; he lived with his wife and four children. He had not come into court on the case against him for many reasons, but now he was preparing himself to go to trial on an allegation that he distributed cocaine.

Gary asked him to focus on the time when he was living at 223 Geneva Avenue. Pablo testified that he was living in Apartment B on the first floor with a woman named Carmen, who was a friend. He was not living with his wife then because they had quarreled and separated. Yes, he remembered being arrested from 223 Geneva Avenue, and yes, he was leaving his first-floor apartment when he was arrested. The night before he was arrested, the police raided Apartment E on the third floor. Watching from a friend's house in the same apartment complex, Pablo saw the officers come out of the building. The next day, as he was leaving his apartment, the police (he called them "agents") showed up, pointed at him, and said, "That's the one."

"What did they do after that?" Gary asked.

"They came and they grabbed me. They took my wallet away. They took me right back to the building. They took me upstairs, up to the third floor. They were saying I was the owner of that apartment, that they wanted me to open up the apartment and that I had keys to open up that apartment."

The interpreter translated, and then Pablo went on, speaking rapidly. "They frisked me. They found a key on me, but that key wouldn't open that apartment. That key belonged to a car where I had been living before. They tried to open that apartment with that key." No, the key did not open the door.

He did not know the officers who arrested him, but later learned their names: "LaFontaine and Fleming." They took his wallet from his pocket as soon as they arrested him. His license was in his wallet, as well as papers from the place he worked. Later Pablo learned that the officers reported finding his license inside Apartment 3E. "Is that true, that it was there, sir?" Gary asked. Pablo shook his head emphatically as he answered no.

"After they were unable to open the third-floor apartment door, what happened at the time of your arrest?"

"They took me down the stairs, and they started hitting me against the wall. Right there, they turned me around. They put the handcuffs on me, and they started hitting me again."

"Were you eventually, sir, taken into custody and charged with distribution of cocaine?"

"That's true. That's what they said."

"Had you ever distributed cocaine out of the apartments of 223 Geneva Avenue?"

"Never."

"Have you ever distributed any drugs out of any location?"

"Never."

Pablo had stayed in the Charles Street jail until he was able to make a reduced bail. "The convicts in the jail and even some of the court officers put a collection together to help me get out of jail," he said. When he got out of jail, he went to live in Dorchester, on Columbus Avenue. At some point, he went back to 223 Geneva Avenue to collect his personal belongings.

"When you went back, did you have occasion to see Officer LaFontaine again?"

"They saw me, yes."

"When you say 'they,' who do you mean?"

"LaFontaine, Fleming, and another police officer, but I don't remember his name."

"Tell us, please, what happened when you saw those three officers the second time."

"I was talking to some friends of mine after I had put my things in the car. And I was talking to them.... That's when the agents that had arrested me entered. They entered. As soon as they saw me, they said, look at him there. They took me. They grabbed me. They took me to where the stairs are...."

The interpreter translated, and Pablo went on, quite agitated. "LaFontaine was there. He came and he hit me. Then Fleming also hit me. And then I said to them, Why are you hitting me? If I got out of jail yesterday, why do you want to bother me now? They said to me, Shut up. You don't have to say anything. They came and took me and they threw me against the floor. They started kicking me; that is, LaFontaine started kicking me first."

Then one of the officers found a knife under the stairs and said, "This is the evidence that we're going to use now." They kept on kicking Pablo, even though the third officer said to LaFontaine, "Let's leave him alone. It's okay now." LaFontaine replied, "Shut up, you don't have anything to do with this," and began jumping up and down on Pablo's back. Pablo was then arrested and charged in Dorchester District Court with assault and battery on police officers. (I remembered the mug shot of Pablo's bruised and swollen face after his arrest.)

"You were found guilty in that case, is that right?"

Pablo, shifting from side to side in the witness chair, answered, "I was found guilty and the officers were found guilty." He was given probation on the charge, and when he failed to meet the terms, he was given another probation period.

"Did you ever appeal the conviction for assaulting those officers?"

"No, I didn't know what to do. I didn't know what to do."

"Do you know Carlos Montilla? This man right here," Gary said, gesturing to Carlos.

"No." And no, he had never seen Carlos Montilla before yesterday in court and had never seen him in the area of 223 Geneva Avenue.

"Sir, are you willing to testify if the judge were to grant Mr. Montilla a new trial?"

"Yes."

"You would testify on Mr. Montilla's behalf at that trial; is that right?"

"Yes."

"Nothing further, Your Honor," Gary said, sitting down.

Beland, whose clothes I had not noticed the day before, was flamboyantly dressed today: white culotte suit, fuchsia blouse, and matching fuchsia shoes. She walked to the microphone at the end of the empty jury box and began to question Pablo. After asking him about his previous failure to come to court, she turned to the evening of the alleged crime. "At around ten o'clock that night you were out in front of the Geneva Avenue apartments?"

"No," Pablo answered. He was in the apartment of some friends in another building, #225.

"Sir, were you outside at all that night?"

"I was in the apartment with my friends."

"You were inside the apartment with your friends at about ten o'clock that night?"

"I don't know if it was ten." With his body twisted to one side, Pablo looked ready to climb out of the witness chair.

"Well, why don't you describe your activities that night," Beland said.

"Well, we were drinking beer. We were watching television."

"Sir, did you tell Mr. Crossen or members from his office when you signed the affidavit that you were outside 223 Geneva Avenue when you saw police enter the building?"

"No," Pablo said, glaring at the prosecutor.

"You didn't tell that to anyone who typed up an affidavit?"

"No."

Beland strode to the witness chair, Pablo's affidavit in her hand. "Sir, I show you a signature and ask if it's your signature."

"Yes, that's my signature."

"And these are the facts that you indicated to Mr. Crossen?"

"Yes."

"Sir, with the translator's assistance, I'm going to ask you to read paragraph one." She turned on her heel and walked away from Pablo, returning to the microphone.

After the interpreter finished reading the paragraph, Pablo said, "I'd like to apologize because I'm a little bit confused because it's been a while since I — I didn't have an opportunity to go over what I was going to say and it's been a while since I —"

Beland cut him off. "Sir, my question to you is which are the correct facts?"

Pablo tapped the paper and said, "This is correct."

"That's correct," Beland said bitingly. "So what you just told the Court for the last hour has been incorrect?"

"Objection," Gary said.

"I'll sustain the objection," Porada said, but Pablo answered anyway, "No, it's not incorrect."

"Sir, isn't it also —"

Pablo interrupted her to explain. "The only thing I was mistaken about was the thing about my being outside when I said that I wasn't outside. And I know that I was outside."

"When you were standing in front of 223 on that night, who else was with you? Who were you talking to?"

"I think I was talking to somebody, but I don't remember very well... I'm very nervous. I'm very nervous, and I think I want to get down from here."

"Sir, were you charged with assault and battery on a police officer?"

"Yes, it's true."

"Before a judge in Dorchester District Court did you admit to those charges?"

"No."

"I have no other questions," Beland said.

Gary, in redirect, asked Pablo to confirm that the night before he was arrested, he spent some time in the apartment at 225 drinking beer and watching television and some time outside in the courtyard, when he saw the police officers coming out of 223.

The judge then excused Pablo: "You may go to work." He said, "Thank you," and sprang from the witness chair. Snatching up his jacket from the bench where Abelow was sitting, he made a beeline out of the courtroom, his attorney hurrying to keep up.

There were no further witnesses, Gary told the judge, but he wanted to offer records from LaFontaine's file on five separate incidents. Assault and battery on a prisoner and lying about it to internal affairs investigators. Violating department rules and making untruthful statements to internal affairs investigators, for which he was fired. Assault and battery of a prisoner with a blackjack, a walkie talkie, and electric shock. Assault and battery of a woman with a dangerous weapon. And the most recent, for which he had been fired: an internal affairs finding of extortion, assault and battery, and lying to investigators.

Gary went through them one by one. Beland objected to each, with Porada sustaining, even though Gary argued that these instances of brutality and lying to police investigators went to the heart of LaFontaine's credibility. At the end, he gave it one more try. "Your Honor, the most difficult aspect of this, as the Court can appreciate, is that we have an officer who took the stand yesterday and took the Fifth Amendment." Gary could not ask LaFontaine questions to show the judge his credibility on the stand, therefore he urged Porada to take into account the officer's record of lying to his own department.

But Porada was firm. "I do feel, even for purposes of this hearing, that evidence should not be before this court. Do you have anything else, Mr. Crossen?"

"Your Honor, we have no further evidence," Gary said, sitting down.

Beland then called Officer Fleming to the stand, for the purpose, she said, of impeaching Pablo Osario. Fleming, in uniform but without a jacket, identified himself and spelled his name. He testified that on the night of the incident, he observed Pablo Osario outside 223 Geneva Avenue engaged in transactions. He already knew Osario and recognized him. At about ten o'clock, his partner, LaFontaine, entered the front of the hallway, and he went to the rear. Pablo was no longer in sight. Later Fleming entered the third-floor apartment, where, he said, "we found several items, like telephone bills, with Pablo Osario's name on it."

Gary objected. "I'm not sure whether Mr. Fleming is testifying from his own personal knowledge or what somebody might have told him." After Porada sustained, Fleming went on, leaning forward to speak directly into the microphone. "I found personal items that belonged to Pablo Osario inside the apartment. And at that time I made out a warrant with Pablo Osario for his arrest for the trafficking."

"Thank you, sir. I have no other questions," Beland said. But she had not asked about Pablo's license, and Fleming did not mention finding it himself.

Mike and Gary whispered together for a minute or two, and then Mike asked a question to confirm that Fleming had not seen Carlos outside with Pablo that night.

"That's correct. Yes."

"That's all I have," Mike said.

Porada, who had swiveled her chair so that she faced Fleming, asked him a question herself. "On the evening in question, did you ever see Mr. Montilla, the defendant in this hearing, in or about the vicinity of 223 Geneva Avenue to the best of your knowledge?"

Fleming began, "About a —"

"I'm sorry, I can't hear," Mike interrupted.

As Fleming leaned toward the microphone, my heart thumped. What was he going to say? It was a simple yes or no question. He spoke slowly and deliberately. "About a half an hour after Al LaFontaine gave a description of the suspect, I went down to Geneva Ave., about half a mile. And I met Carlos Montilla for the first time."

I met Carlos Montilla for the first time! Fleming was telling the judge in so many words that he knew it wasn't Carlos there that night with Pablo.

"Thank you, Officer. You may step down."

The Commonwealth had nothing more, and there was a five-minute recess before closing arguments. Evelin hurried out of the courtroom, but I remained seated, and Mike came over to talk to me. "Well, Fleming hurt Pablo, but not Carlos," he said. "He went further than his trial testimony."

"Yes, he as much as said it wasn't Carlos at all. I think he was trying to help Carlos."

Mike shook his head, his brow furrowed. "If we lose this, I'm going to take the gloves off and go public. What was the police department thinking of — using LaFontaine as a witness again and again, knowing his record?"

When the recess was over, Evelin still hadn't returned. Belliveau, who had also gone outside, came in alone. After a few minutes, Evelin slipped into the courtroom and sat down in the row behind me. Throughout Gary's closing arguments, tears ran down her face.

nineteen

GARY STOOD FOR A MOMENT looking down at his notes, pen in hand; then he dropped the pen and placed his hands on his hips, hooking his index fingers over his belt. "Your Honor, I have wrestled in trying to put together an argument for you, to figure out what rationale an officer would have for making up a story against a man."

If an officer breaks into an apartment without a search warrant, he has to have a reason. LaFontaine's reason, Gary suggested, was a fleeing felon, a story he made up after the fact to justify going into the apartment where he suspected drugs. The officer testified to a scene that was highly improbable, as the judge could see from the trial transcript given to her yesterday. "I am sure you will review the transcript, if you haven't already had the opportunity."

Judge Porada, her head cocked to one side quizzically, paid close attention to Gary's words.

Gary went on about the improbability of LaFontaine's testimony: the photographs introduced into evidence would show LaFontaine's observations were impossible given the physical surroundings of the apartment house. "He couldn't have made the observations that he made with three men standing in front of that door." He couldn't have knocked into the door, as he testified at the second trial, while the three men were there. "They hadn't moved, and you'll see that in the transcript. And he said he hit the door before they even ran away."

Here was an officer, Gary argued, who didn't arrest anyone at the scene, although with his gun drawn he was in a perfect position to arrest all four individuals. LaFontaine then testified that Mr. Montilla, the man in the red striped underwear, "gets out of that apartment in some improbable fashion. And the Court has to believe, if it credits his testimony, that he went out that kitchen window and either jumped or scaled. And I suggest to you that on all the facts that's highly improbable even if his testimony weren't subject to the various forms of impeachment that it is. But the reason he did it was to justify the lack of a search warrant because he wanted the courts to believe that he was chasing a fleeing felon."

The judge heard the testimony of Pablo Osario today, Gary said, and of the witness that Ms. Beland put on the stand to discredit him. "But quite frankly, that witness did not go a long way towards discrediting Mr. Osario. And he made it quite clear that he never saw Mr. Montilla anywhere in the vicinity of 223 Geneva Avenue. He only saw him for the first time after he had been arrested by the arresting officers. Yet he was the surveillance officer with Officer LaFontaine at the scene." Even Ms. Beland said that Fleming could not identify Mr. Montilla, only Officer LaFontaine could.

"Your Honor is as familiar as I am or anyone with what the Appeals Court and the Supreme Court have to say about the inherent unreliability of single-witness identification cases." With his right hand, Gary gestured toward Carlos: "This man sits in jail and sits subject to a deportation proceeding as a result of that inherently unreliable single-witness identification."

Gary said he didn't want to go over all the evidence, but wanted to review some of what the judge had heard. She would see in the transcript of the first trial that Officer LaFontaine testified that the kitchen window opened up and down, not side to side. "You'll also see that he avoided testifying to that in the second trial and only identified a window." In fact, as she would see from the photographs, the window opened side to side making it "highly improbable that anybody could have escaped through it off into the night and gotten away."

The judge would also see that twenty or thirty minutes after he was supposed to have leaped out the window wearing only underpants, Mr. Montilla was found dressed nearly a mile away at the social club where he was arrested. "I submit to you that is highly improbable on the face of it. But with the further evidence that's been gathered as a result of the post-trial investigation, it is completely lacking in any credibility whatsoever."

LaFontaine also testified that he looked through the stairs and made observations. "He didn't look through the stairs, Your Honor. He couldn't look through the stairs. It's physically impossible to look through the stairs."

Pablo Osario testified under oath today, at risk of incriminating himself, and he said that he does not know Carlos Montilla. "What's his motive for telling that to the Court under oath? I suggest his only motive is to tell you the truth. He doesn't have anything to gain, Your Honor." He came into court of his own free will, not under subpoena, and he did his best to testify truthfully to the facts, Gary said.

With respect to the relationship with Dolores, the defendant was hamstrung as to finding out more: "The man who accused him won't answer our questions at this stage. And that gets me into the invocation of the Fifth Amendment by Officer LaFontaine."

There has to be a consequence, Gary argued, to the prosecution's one and only material witness taking the Fifth Amendment. He asked the judge either to draw an adverse inference against the government or to consider LaFontaine's testimony as stricken for the sake of her decision on the motion for a new trial.

Gary's voice became more urgent: "You've got a young man here, first conviction, serving a prison term. He has three children and a wife. He's going to face deportation, and he's facing it on the strength of what I suggest to you is the weakest of cases. If you look at the trial transcripts, you will see that it just hinges on the one man."

Gary paused and then made his final plea: "I would ask you as a matter of fundamental fairness to grant the motion and let Mr. Montilla have another opportunity to try this case. Thank you, Your Honor."

It was Beland's turn. This time she did not move to the microphone but stood at the prosecutor's table. The Commonwealth's position, she began, was that there was no basis for a new trial to be granted. The jury that convicted the defendant saw what the scene looked like, what the hallway looked like.

As she spoke, Beland gestured with both hands, first toward the witness stand and then toward the judge, as if she were performing aerobics without music, her broad shoulders moving up and down. Judge Porada sat up straight, leaning back a little, less attentive now.

Everything had been presented to the jury, Beland argued. "The only thing now which is coming before the court, I suggest, is the fact that the witness, Officer LaFontaine, now has some other problems." Those problems were long after anything to do with Carlos Montilla and were not admissible material to impeach the witness.

"All legal and all fairness and all rules were followed, and the case was presented to the jury. And there is not anything different now that was not presented to them." Beland sounded put-upon and sarcastic. "The Commonwealth's position is the jury made the decision. All that is being done now is saying give us another chance. Well, Your Honor, the court system doesn't work that way. So, Your Honor, the Commonwealth is asking you to deny the motion for a new trial."

Judge Porada spoke abruptly, cutting the prosecutor off: "I'll take it under advisement. I expect to have a decision in the next week or so."

We all stood as Porada left the courtroom, and then I hurried to Evelin in the row behind me. I put my arm around her and leaned my head against hers. When Mike and Gary came over to us, we were both weeping.

There was nothing to do now but wait, and I tried to prepare myself for whatever happened. I took long walks along the river, where the trees were just beginning to show buds, amber tips that looked like a sunset glow. I kept thinking of the words of the father in *The Winslow Boy*, which I had recently seen on television. On the eve of his son's hearing, Mr. Winslow (played by Gordon Jackson) says, "I don't know what I shall do if we lose."

What would I do if we lost? Would I be too cast down to go on? Would I have the heart to pursue one last card and try to get a pardon for Carlos? A long week passed without any word. Every time the phone rang in the bookstore, my heart beat faster. I willed myself to be calm, to accept what came, to go on from there.

On Sunday March 11, I went with friends to see Sarah Caldwell's production of *The Magic Flute.* In the opera's final ecstatic scenes, the lovers Tamino and Pamina, protected by the magic flute and their love for each other, survive their trial by fire and water. The Queen of the Night and her accomplices are vanquished before the sunlight of Wisdom and Truth. The exultant chorus sings that light has triumphed over darkness, and hate is turned to kindness.

Caught up in Mozart's joy, I was elated at the victory of good over evil. Was it a sign? Or just a fairy tale that had nothing to do with the real world?

❧

The call came at three o'clock on Tuesday afternoon, March 13, ten long days after the hearing. I was alone in the bookstore, shelving a new novel in the hardcover fiction section when the phone rang. I knew before I answered who it was.

"Hello, Linda, it's Mike."

I could not tell anything from his tone. "Yes?" I said, barely breathing.

"And I have Gary on the line with me."

Then I knew. Elation and adrenaline shot through me. "It's good news!"

"Victory!" Mike said, triumph now clear in his voice.

"Hallelujah! I thought if it was good news, you'd both call, and if it was bad, you'd flip a coin to see who had to do it."

Mike laughed and said, quoting, "Victory has a thousand parents; defeat is an orphan." We made a plan to meet an hour later at the African Meeting House on Beacon Hill, where the Foley, Hoag foundation was holding its annual awards ceremony, so that I could get a copy of the ruling.

I was still flying. "When can Carlos come home?" I asked.

"There will be a bail hearing on Monday, and unless there's some hitch, he'll be released then."

I did a quick victory dance around the bookstore and then called Evelin at her office. "Oh, my God," she said, "Oh, my God," repeating it over and over, "Oh, my God," and then, "I've got to go. I'm going to tell him in person."

But nothing in this case went without a hitch. In her dash to the prison, she just missed the 4:30 end of visiting hours and had to wait until six, sitting alone in the anteroom. Carlos was in the gym when he was notified that he had a visitor. Thinking it might be Mike or Gary, he took a shower before coming out. It was close to seven by then, more than two hours since Evelin's happy arrival; she was tired and the first rush of excitement had faded. When she told him the news he did not believe it.

He hugged her, almost crying, asking again and again, "Are you sure? Are you sure?" And he was full of worry. "How can I pay back Mike and Gary? I can't ever earn enough money to pay them. And what am I going to do about Linda? How can I ever thank her?" He went on and on, distraught, nervous, and unable to believe his ordeal was coming to an end.

I had a long list of people to call, beginning with my mother, and I used the same opening line each time: "Do you have any champagne in the house?" Everyone was thrilled; everyone had extravagant praise for me. One friend compared me to Joe Montana, another to Joan of Arc. I preferred Joe to Joan, but I was deeply touched by the feelings behind the words.

Before going to bed that night, I reread several times my copy of Judge Porada's five-page "findings, rulings and order on defendant's motion for a new trial." After a summary of the case, she wrote, "Based upon the affidavits submitted, the oral evidence presented at the hearing on the defendant's motion for a new trial, and the transcripts of the defendant's trials, the court makes the following findings:

1. If Carlos Montilla was present in the third floor apartment at 223 Geneva Avenue, in Dorchester, Massachusetts, when Officer LaFontaine entered the same, Carlos Montilla did not exit the third floor apartment from either the front or rear door.

2. That if the defendant exited from the third floor apartment kitchen window as testified to by Officer LaFontaine at the defendant's first trial, the defendant would have had no access to the roof. The only access available to the defendant from that window would have been to the ground by jumping from the third floor to the ground which would necessarily have resulted in serious injury to him.

3. That Officer LaFontaine from his vantage point on the second floor could not have made the observations of Carlos Montilla within the third floor apartment to which Officer LaFontaine testified.

4. That all of the above contained in findings 1 through 3 could have been known to the defendant at the time of his trial in July, 1988 or October, 1988 and would not constitute newly discovered evidence.

5. That Pablo Osario who lived at 223 Geneva Avenue in Dorchester, Massachusetts, was charged as a co-defendant with Carlos Montilla. At the time of defendant's trials in July 1988 and October 1988, Pablo Osario was in default and a fugitive from justice. The whereabouts of Pablo Osario were unknown.

6. If Pablo Osario had been available as a witness to the defendant at the time of his trials, he would have testified that he did not know Carlos Montilla and had never seen him on or about the premises at 223 Geneva Avenue in Dorchester where Pablo Osario had been a resident.

7. The testimony of Pablo Osario would have been the weakest kind of evidence to be offered to a fact-finder because Pablo Osario was a co-defendant. Nevertheless, Pablo Osario's testimony would have buttressed Mr. Montilla's testimony that he was not present at 223 Geneva Avenue in Dorchester, Massachusetts, at the time of the alleged incident which was the subject matter of his arrest. Pablo Osario's testimony would have constituted newly discovered evidence."

The eighth finding was that Carlos had indeed had a relationship with Dolores. "However, this relationship occurred in December 1986 and would not in any way form the basis for a motive on the part of Officer LaFontaine to arrest Carlos Montilla." And with this sentence Judge Porada dismissed as irrelevant all the time, effort, and money that we put into establishing the Dolores connection.

The ninth finding dealt with LaFontaine's appearance at the hearing on the motion for a new trial: "...the only information that Officer LaFontaine would furnish was his name and address and claimed the privilege of self-incrimination under the federal and state constitutions. Officer LaFontaine is presently under indictment and awaiting trial in Suffolk Superior Court on charges arising out of a drug investigation."

In the section headed <u>RULINGS,</u> Porada wrote, "Based upon the totality of the foregoing, the Court finds that substantial doubt has been cast upon the veracity of the testimony offered by Officer LaFontaine at the time of the defendant's trial. This court cannot leave unnoticed that Officer LaFontaine, with respect to the subject matter of this hearing, refused to answer all relevant questions based upon his claim of the privilege against self-incrimination. These factors coupled with the availability now of the testimony of Pablo Osario who is willing to testify at Mr. Montilla's trial that he had never seen him before the hearing on the motion for a new trial and had not seen him on the premises at 223 Geneva Avenue in Dorchester, Massachusetts, in the interests of justice, warrants a new trial."

And finally, the order: "The motion for a new trial is <u>ALLOWED.</u> The convictions of Carlos M. Montilla ... are set aside...."

Later, I lay in bed unable to sleep, exhausted but exhilarated. Certain words repeated over and over in my mind: in the interests of justice, the motion is allowed, in the interests of justice...

Shortly after ten the next morning Gary called me in the bookstore. I began to tell him how great he was, but he cut me off. "Time to talk about nuts and bolts," he said. In particular, bail. We needed to be prepared to get our hands on a thousand dollars. Gary was trying to reach Lynn Beland to ascertain her position. "They may argue he's more of an escape risk, but we'd counter that he's substantially less. We'll shoot for personal recognizance, but we need to be prepared for cash bail." He had called Evelin to find out what it was last time: $500. If the bail was met, Carlos would be released from the courthouse after the hearing. "He's now a pretrial detainee, not a convicted felon," Gary said.

Fortunately, Gary's words registered, to come back later when I needed them: *a pretrial detainee, not a convicted felon.*

Carlos was very nervous about the bail hearing. He kept asking Evelin, "Am I really going home on Monday? Should I give away my clothes?" It was considered bad luck to take your clothes with you when you left prison.

I was nervous too. On Monday morning I awoke at three and could not go back to sleep. I lay in bed and gazed through the lace-curtained windows at the shadows of trees moving outside, cast by a neighbor's patio light. Now and then I closed my eyes, but sleep did not come. When the clock radio came on at 7:15, playing classical music, I was wide awake.

Carlos, asleep on his prison cot, also woke at three o'clock, I learned later. Alone in the dark cell, he turned on the light over his bed (as always, by tightening the bare bulb) and began to read his Spanish Bible. At five, when the guards came to wake him, he was already dressed and ready to go.

twenty

I WAS THE FIRST OF our group to arrive outside courtroom 705, where the usual assortment of lawyers and defendants milled around waiting for the first session to begin. A few minutes later came Evelin and Neftalee, Carlos's brother, carrying little Carlos in his arms. Neftalee was younger than Carlos but bigger and taller, with a darker complexion. Like Carlos, he had a shy, engaging smile, which he flashed at me when Evelin introduced us. Evelin had $500 in cash with her, borrowed from Carlos's mother. If we needed more, I would go to the bank for a cashier's check drawn from my savings.

Promptly at 9:30 both Mike and Gary arrived. Mike had rearranged his schedule to be there, and I was delighted to see him. He and I sat down on one of the benches while Gary went inside the courtroom. He came out twenty minutes later and beckoned to us; Evelin, Mike, and I joined him in a huddle off to the side. "Here's what's happening," he said. Lynn Beland was not in, and the Commonwealth was asking to kick it over one day. We would oppose that, but if we didn't prevail, Carlos would have to spend the night in the Charles Street Jail.

"The night he spent there during the hearing was the worst night of his life," I told Mike and Gary, repeating something Evelin had just told me two days before. "Some big guy beat up on him and tried to take his wedding ring."

"He was in a cell with other people?" Gary asked.

"Yes," Evelin answered, "but then they said, 'He's state property,' and put him by himself."

Shortly after ten o'clock we went into the courtroom, Gary and Mike gathering with the other lawyers in front, while Evelin, Neftalee, and I sat in a middle row of the spectators' section. This courtroom, where the first session was held every morning, was similar to the other courtrooms but much larger. The atmosphere was one of barely controlled chaos, with much murmuring and milling around. The magistrate (in tweed jacket, no robes) was trying to get at least one case cleared for trial that morning. He had a judge waiting, he said, but all the cases were continued.

When Carlos's case was called, Assistant D.A. Jim Coffey, substituting for Beland who was away from the office that day, asked for a postponement. Gary objected, saying that Beland had received a week's notice of this hearing. "My client had substantial difficulty the last time he was in Charles Street Jail, and his wife has taken the day off from her job as a legal secretary to be here."

The magistrate, who had handled the previous cases with brisk impatience, peppered by wisecracks, wasted no time: "I've read the findings and see no reason to put off the bail hearing." He then ordered the case to room 702.

That room, tucked away in a side corridor, was quite small, with only two rows of benches. Evelin and I sat in the back row, right behind Mike and Gary. (Neftalee was out in the hall with little Carlos, as no children were allowed inside.) Jim Coffey, the tall, pale young man subbing for Beland, came in and sat down next to Gary. He asked to see the judge's ruling, read it, handed it back, and left the room.

When the three cases ahead of us were disposed of, Carlos was brought in by a guard. He looked quite spiffy in a black jacket and pants and a white shirt. Between his cuffed hands he carried a manila envelope. In contrast to the scruffy fellows who had gone before him, Carlos was immaculate. He beamed at Evelin and me, a closed-lip smile that curved into his cheeks and shone out of his eyes. He sat down at the table with his lawyers, and Mike gave him a nudge of encouragement.

Carlos's case was called, and Gary stood up. "Gary Crossen for the defendant," and then Mike, "And Mike Keating for the defendant." The judge raised his eyebrows slightly in surprise. This was a simple bail hearing, and the three previous defendants had shared two public defenders. Robert Mulligan, known to be a law-and-order judge, had rugged good looks, with salt-and-pepper hair and a dark moustache. While we waited for the assistant D.A., he read Gary's copy of the ruling, since the clerk was having difficulty finding the court's copy in the overstuffed file.

Coffey finally returned, and the judge asked Gary what the bail was last time. Gary said, "It was $500, Your Honor, and Mr. Montilla showed up for both his previous trials. His wife is here today to take him home."

Presenting the prosecution's side, Coffey told the judge that the Commonwealth had another witness against Carlos, a police officer who had found his license in the apartment. (Coffey had obviously dashed out to see what else the Commonwealth had for a case and confused Carlos with Pablo.) He asked for $10,000 cash bail or $100,000 surety.

"I've read the findings," Mulligan said, "and if anything he's less of a risk than before, because the Commonwealth's case is weaker. I see no reason for any higher bail than last time." Addressing Mike and Gary, he asked if that was acceptable.

"We were hoping for less, Your Honor, but it's acceptable," Gary answered, "and Mr. Montilla's wife has the $500 with her."

Mulligan duly set bail for $500, and Carlos was taken out of the room, still in handcuffs. The rest of us — Gary, Mike, Evelin, and I — trooped down the hall to the clerk's office. Carlos's brother, Neftalee, who had been pacing the halls, now showed up with little Carlos asleep on his shoulder. It was just after eleven o'clock.

Evelin handed me a white envelope with the money inside. "You hold it," she said. "I'm too nervous."

We were waiting for someone to help us in the clerk's office when Mike said, "It's a good thing we didn't have to wait until tomorrow. It's like *Bonfire of the Vanities* — you never know what can happen once you get caught up in the system. One more night in jail and God knows what they'd throw at him next." *They*, I gathered, included those on both sides of the judicial fence.

Already late for a meeting, Mike and Gary had to leave before the clerk got around to us. When it was our turn, I handed Evelin the envelope, and she gave it to the clerk, who took out the money, counted it, and gave her a receipt. On the counter we saw the manila envelope that contained Carlos's papers; his address was listed as 223 Geneva Avenue. "What is this?" Evelin said in frustration. "He told them his address."

"LaFontaine did that to make it look worse for Carlos. It was part of his..." I struggled for the right word.

"Part of his scheme," Evelin finished for me.

"Exactly. Part of his scheme." Or his malice.

We had an hour's wait, and Evelin treated us to lunch at a cafeteria across the plaza from the courthouse. "I'm really tired," I told her as we finished our meal. "I woke up at three."

"I woke up at four-thirty," she said.

"Who's nervous? Not us," I joked, and we laughed a bit raggedly.

After finishing lunch, we lingered outside in the brick plaza. It was a beautiful sunny day, with a sweet breeze. Little Carlos chased the pigeons, squealing with delight as they flapped into the air.

We were back at the courtroom promptly at one, and Evelin went inside to check. After a minute or two, she came charging out the swinging door like a Fury bursting on stage: "They can't release him because of the immigration thing. We forgot about the detainer!"

I hurried into the courtroom to see for myself, and with Evelin close behind me, I marched up to the stall where the court officer, a tall, baby-faced young man, was sitting. "Excuse me, but can you please explain what's happening?" I asked. A bit surprised at my presence, the court officer returned courtesy with courtesy. "There's a federal warrant on him from Immigration," he said, "and they can't release him."

Gary's words came back to me. "His attorney says he's no longer a convicted felon," I said. "He's a pretrial detainee. He's been released on bail, and his wife has a receipt." I looked toward Evelin, who nodded silently. She seemed numb with disbelief. This was supposed to be over.

"Is that the only reason he has a detainer, because he's a convicted felon?"

"Yes, that's the only reason, and the conviction has been overturned."

"Okay, I'll make some calls," he said, lifting the phone in front of him.

An hour later we learned that Immigration was coming at three o'clock to take Carlos for a hearing at the federal courthouse. Evelin was frantic. "He'll die when he sees the Immigration people," she said. "He won't know what's happening." We all stood at a pay phone as I called Gary at his office. "There's no point in your waiting there," he said. "Come on over here." The federal courthouse was right next to Foley, Hoag in Post Office Square.

We had already pushed the elevator button when we saw the court officer hurrying toward us from the other end of the hall. "Immigration doesn't want him after all," he said when he reached us. "All we need now is instructions on what to do with the federal warrant. They may tell us just to tear it up. I'll see what I can do." He was surprisingly kind.

"That was good timing," Evelin said to me. "We would have been gone in another minute."

"We should have had such luck long ago," I said.

By now we were used to long waits and settled ourselves, more or less patiently, on the bench nearest the courtroom, at right angles to the wall and facing away from the door. I sat sideways so I could rest my elbow on the back of the bench and my head on my hand. Evelin, Neftalee, and little Carlos faced forward, and I was the only who could see the courtroom door. I closed my eyes, exhausted, and almost fell asleep. The sound of the courtroom door opening startled me awake. There was the tall court officer, and next to him, like a dazed child being returned to his family, stood Carlos.

"Here he is," the court officer said, smiling.

And there he was.

We were stunned. Evelin was the first to react, jumping up and running to embrace him. They held each other tight for a long time, wordless, their heads pressed together. Next, Carlos embraced his brother, and they too held each other a long time. Then he bent down to greet his son, who sat on the bench looking up in silent astonishment. It was the first time in eighteen months the little boy had seen his father outside prison.

Last, Carlos turned to me, and we embraced. He spoke to me in Spanish and Evelin translated: "I can't express all I'm feeling right now. I don't know how I can ever thank you. I've come out of hell."

"I'm so happy too. Why am I the only one crying?" I said. The tears had started the moment I saw him.

"He's just holding it all in," Evelin said.

"I'm exhausted," Carlos explained. "I woke up at three this morning."

"Linda woke up at three too," Evelin told him, and he and I smiled at each other. The bond between us was stronger than ever.

Going down in the elevator, Carlos leaned wearily against Evelin. Neftalee carried little Carlos, who continued to gaze at his father in amazement. We went out the door that had "Justice for All" etched above it and walked into dazzling sunlight. Gesturing to the bright blue sky, I touched Carlos's shoulder. "This is a beautiful spring day just for Carlos."

We all laughed, and then I asked him, "How do you feel?"

"I feel *beautiful!*" Carlos exclaimed in English.

Evelin corrected him: "You feel very good."

"No," I said. "Beautiful is just right."

"We've gone through two cases of champagne," Ed whispered to me as he made another round to refill glasses. "We're into private stock now." The DeMores' elegant double drawing room was packed with thirty-five happy people celebrating Carlos's release from prison.

Carlos and Evelin stood in front of one of the fireplaces, receiving the congratulations of strangers. Carlos, looking like a nightclub singer, wore white pants and a fitted white jacket with black satin lapels. Evelin was in white too, a dress with a V-neck and gold buttons. Josua stood in front of Evelin, and she had one hand on his chest and the other linked through Carlos's arm. Carlos held one-year-old Neftalee, who stayed awake all evening. Upstairs, in one of the DeMores' bedrooms, little Carlos was fast asleep in his miniature tuxedo and white shoes. Except for that one missing child, too tired to socialize, the Montilla family tableau was complete.

Evelin was like a shy, gracious protector of her husband, who looked dazed and overwhelmed. They had brought with them Carlos's cousin Anna and his aunt Hilda, but the only other people they already knew were Ed, Mike, Gary, Claudia the volunteer translator, and me. Only one guest, a foreign-language teacher, could speak Spanish. Mike and Gary's wives were there, but Gerry Belliveau came alone and left early. The rest of the crowd was a mix of some of my best friends, Beacon Hill neighbors, and Ed and Paula's friends, one of whom was a priest, wearing mufti that evening.

Not everyone who had climbed aboard the nobility train, as Ed put it, was able to come to the party, and few of those who were there had known each other before. It was a laughing, happy, jubilant crowd that evening, but there were some quiet tears as well. Mike's wife, Marty, got tears in her eyes when she saw how Carlos had dressed up for the occasion. Another woman, who told me that she had donated for philosophical reasons and did not expect to be emotionally moved at the party, found herself tearing up as she looked at Carlos and his family. "It was the children that did it," she said.

At about nine o'clock, as some people were getting ready to leave, Ed called everyone to attention. He had a few words to say. Everyone in the crowded double drawing room, with some people looking in from the hall, quieted down. Ed stood near Carlos by the fireplace, with me next to him, all three of us holding champagne glasses.

Ed began with a joke: "I'll tell you one thing I've learned from this. Don't go into the bookstore around the holidays unless you're prepared to get involved in a cause. That time of year I'm in the mood to say yes to anything." Laughing, I reassured him, "Don't worry — no more causes for a while. You're safe."

More serious now, Ed went on. "As I look around this room, I'm struck by the diversity of the group Linda's courage and persistence brought together. People responded in many ways: Mike and Gary who represented Carlos without charge, Claudia, who helped us by going to the prison to translate, others of you who made donations to help someone you didn't even know. It was that diverse human touch that got results. An injustice was reversed, and Carlos is home with his family, all because of what one person set in motion."

Ed turned to me and lifted his glass, "I want to toast Linda and Carlos and his family and all of you who came together to help."

That toast drunk, it was my turn to speak. I hoped that the right words would come, that I could say truly what was in my mind and heart. Like Ed, I began on a light note. "When I staggered out of that jury room almost two years ago, I thought that was it. Who could have foreseen all this? It was my first jury duty, and probably my last. I asked Gary if the D.A.'s office has a blacklist for jurors, and he said yes, but there's only one name on it."

When the laughter died down, I turned to Ed. "None of this could have happened without you, Ed. You were the vital link in a chain of trust. I believed in Carlos" — I put my hand on his shoulder — "and Ed believed in me. He brought in Mike, and Mike brought in Gary."

Looking toward Mike and Gary, who were standing together by the door into the hall, I said, "Ed and Mike and Gary are real heroes, true white knights. And Carlos couldn't have had better lawyers at any price. I've told them that if gratitude could be banked, they'd be millionaires. They could live on the interest."

"Never touch the principal," someone added, and we all laughed.

I became serious, and my listeners were quiet. "Last October someone told me, 'You're wasting your time. The system doesn't work. You should have spent your money on a well-placed bribe.' That kind of cynicism chilled me to the heart. It so completely missed the point of what we were trying to do."

Looking around, I said, "There are no cynics in this room." Smiling, I added, "There may be a few skeptics, and we are grateful to them, especially Gary, who was a much-needed balance to the cock-eyed optimists." Gary touched his forehead and tipped his hand to me in a salute.

With the faces of friends old and new watching me, I became serious again, my heart in my voice. "Tonight we are celebrating a great victory. It's not just a victory over injustice. It's a victory over cynicism, a celebration of what's best in people. I think it's truly astounding how all of you rallied to help a young man you did not know. I toast you all."

We lifted our glasses and drank. It was a rare moment, one of pure, undiluted joy, and I savored it for several sweet seconds. "I must tell you that at Carlos and Evelin's wedding in prison, we drank our toasts with Orange Crush from the vending machine. This tastes much better."

A friend took a photo of Carlos and me in front of the fireplace. He put his arm around my shoulder, saying, "My second mother," and we both laughed. The flashbulb, like a surge of sunshine, lit up the room.

As people began to leave, Gary and I talked for the first time that evening. He confessed that the Carlos case was an eye-opener for him. "I never sent anyone to jail who I wasn't convinced was guilty. I believed that people who were in prison belonged there."

"I think there was a purpose in this for all of us," I said. "For Mike it was a chance to reconnect with his idealism as a young lawyer. For you I think it was a chance to see things from the other side."

"And you?" he asked teasingly. "What was the purpose for you?"

I paused before answering. "It opened my eyes too. I was going along in my safe little world with blinders on, and I was in danger of becoming — I don't know — complacent, set in my ways. This shook me up. I had never put my whole heart and soul into anything before. And in a way, it's set me free from myself."

"You make it sound like Carlos saved you instead of the other way around."

"Maybe we saved each other," I said.

Gary raised an eyebrow. "Maybe. Who knows?"

"Right," I agreed. "Who knows?"

epilogue

THREE MONTHS AFTER CARLOS'S RELEASE from prison, on June 6, 1990, a seven-woman, five-man jury, including a priest, found LaFontaine guilty of two counts of attempted extortion and one count of larceny. He was acquitted of the assault and battery charges.

During the four-day trial, witnesses for the prosecution testified that LaFontaine and his partner not only stole money but helped themselves to a VCR, jewelry, and clothes, including leather pants and a fur coat. LaFontaine "stockpiled" the items while his partner covered everyone with his revolver. During the siege, a witness said, the policemen poured champagne and brandy for their victims. The defense called no witnesses.

Three weeks later LaFontaine was sentenced to four-and-a-half to six years, of which he had to serve at least three. His partner, who had been on the force for only three months at the time of the incident, received a lighter sentence. They remained free for two years pending appeal, but in July 1992, their final appeal having been denied, both were incarcerated.

When he heard about LaFontaine's guilty verdict, Carlos said, "He doesn't know what it's like in prison. Maybe when he's there, he'll remember me and what he did to me." Carlos said this, amazingly, without malice.

In spite of LaFontaine's conviction, the Commonwealth was determined to try Carlos again. Lynn Beland told Gary, "I convinced twenty-three out of twenty-four people he was guilty, and I'm not going to walk away from it now." (Apparently she was as stubborn as I am.) It did not seem to matter that the only witness against Carlos was the man that another attorney in the D.A.'s office had successfully prosecuted. A trial date of June 14 was postponed until August 9.

To our surprise, when the day came, Beland did not press for another continuance, nor was she prepared to go to trial. Mike Keating hurriedly wrote out by hand a motion for dismissal "for want of prosecution," as did Arnold Abelow, still representing Pablo Osario. (Pablo was there with a young man who looked remarkably like Carlos except he had no moustache. Was he the man that LaFontaine saw with Pablo the night of the alleged crime?) Beland looked very unhappy but did not protest, and Judge Grabau granted both motions. The charges against Carlos Montilla and his co-defendant, Pablo Osario, were dismissed.

For their work on the Montilla case and other projects, Foley Hoag was awarded the Massachusetts Bar Association's 1990 pro bono award for law firms. Without the superb legal assistance provided by Foley, Hoag, Carlos would have had no resources to fight his unjust conviction and imprisonment.

On April 1, 1990, the Sunday after the victory party, the *Boston Globe* ran a front-page story with a color photograph of Carlos,

Evelin, and me; the headline read "A lone juror holds out, aids quest for freedom." It was a long story, continued inside for almost a full page. For the first time I learned that Carlos had talked about me to other inmates as "the angel God put in my path." I was also touched by Evelin's words: "She's been like a mom, a friend, and a sister. She was always there for us."

Five weeks later, after returning from a second, more difficult trek in Nepal, I agreed to an interview with Karen Tumulty, a staff reporter for the *Los Angeles Times* who was based in New York and had seen the *Globe* story. Tumulty's story appeared on the front page of the Sunday L.A. *Times* on Memorial Day weekend, and afterwards, we were besieged by film producers who wanted our life-story rights.

"Hollywood wants to make this another woman-in-jeopardy story," I complained to my friend Anne. "They'd love to have LaFontaine holding a knife to my throat." Anne shook her head. "That's not how you were at risk. You put your personhood on the line; you did it with your whole self. That's what was in danger. That was the knife at your throat."

Although I did not expect Hollywood to see it as Anne did, I thought the story was important and should be told. I was hopeful that it could be handled with integrity. We narrowed down forty proposals to six finalists, and after face-to-face meetings, some in L.A., some in Boston, we chose the one we thought was best and signed an option. Later when negotiations broke down over the final contract, I felt both disappointment and relief.

People often ask me, Did you ever hear from the other jurors? The answer is no, even though some of them must have seen the *Boston Globe* story. I can understand why they were not eager to talk to me, and if the shoe were on the other foot, I probably would not have sought them out. After all, I followed my conscience, just as they did. They put their trust in the prosecution and assumed all was proper and aboveboard. Ralph even had said about LaFontaine, "If he weren't a good honest cop, we would have heard testimony about suspensions." With that kind of presumption on its side, the prosecution had an unfair advantage against the young Hispanic who could not speak English. Dorothy summed it up when she said, justifying her guilty vote, "I have to go with *our* side."

Carlos's ordeal left permanent scars. He will never forget the eighteen months he spent in prison for something he did not do, and it troubled him deeply that twenty-three out of twenty-four jurors voted to convict him. "Why did they want to send me to jail when there wasn't any evidence?" he asked me. There was no good answer to give him.

A few months after he was released from prison, Carlos wrote another letter to me:

> My dear Linda,
> I want to send my greatings to you and say how thankfull I am for everything you have done for me. You are a person that allways will shine in my heart and my thoughts. Because you got me out of a place that was very dark. Thank God for your inteligence and kindness.
>
> Linda, I feel so happy for all that you have done for me. You are the reason I am back with my family that I was missing so much. Everything is looking beautiful, and to be together again with my dear wife, and my children I love so much and to see my brother, father, and mother I will never forget.
>
> I am happy to be out of a place where only God and I know what I lived through. The prison. After 18 months away from

*civilisation, all I was thinking about was of a new job as fast as
possible and give back to my family the warm my kids lost from me.
I don't know how to thankfull your kindness, but one thing is for
sure, you will allways be in my heart and mind for the rest of my life.*

And he in mine.

Carlos and Evelin had a little girl, Evelis, born on New Year's
Day 1991. She was so beautiful that Carlos did not want Evelin
to leave her alone in the nursery, for fear someone would steal
her. The baby's birth was a joyous time in a marriage that had
its ups and downs. Although clearly devoted to each other,
things were not easy for Carlos and Evelin after his release from
prison. He had nightmares and showed signs of post-traumat-
ic stress. It was a source of friction and a wound to Carlos's
macho pride that Evelin was still the main breadwinner, earning an excellent salary, and Carlos could only find low-paying
jobs and sometimes went for long periods without steady work.
He hoped to finish his high-school degree so that he could
do better for himself and his family. "I'm trying to grow up,"
he told me. An excellent cook, he dreamed of having his own
restaurant someday.

On an outing to the Public Garden in the summer of 1992,
I took a photograph of the family that hangs in a frame on my
bedroom wall. They stand on the bridge over the Swan Pond,
leaning against the pale-blue wrought iron railing. Behind them
is a sun-dappled weeping willow; in the water below, a swan
boat filled with passengers heads homeward. Carlos, Evelin,
and Josua face the camera. Evelis, who is squirming in her
father's arms, Carlos Jr., and Neftalee look off to the side, their
attention caught by something unseen. The photo is filled with

love and sunshine, and Carlos and Evelin both have radiant smiles. A bright future seems to lie ahead for a warm and happy family. I look at that picture now with some sadness.

I remained close to the family for several years, but then we lost touch. In December 2008 Evelin called me, saying I had been much on her mind, and I learned that there was no fairy-tale ending to their story. They were no longer married, and Evelin had taken back her maiden name. Carlos had been deported to the Dominican Republic about nine years before. During a time when he and Evelin were temporarily separated, he had gotten a ride with someone who had drugs in the car, and both men were arrested and later convicted. "They were not his drugs," Evelin told me emphatically. Carlos was in prison for a year and then deported. "I had to divorce him," Evelin said, "but I didn't want to."

Carlos and Evelin talk all the time, she told me, and the children visit him every summer. He works at a hotel, doing low-level jobs, sometimes selling bottles of water on the beach. "I'm afraid he will never grow up," Evelin said. The children are all doing well. Josua is married and has two children. Carlos Jr. is an artist who has won prizes for his work; he hopes to attend an art college. The three children — Carlos Jr., Neftalee, and Evelis — live with Evelin in a small town in eastern Massachusetts.

I do not know the real story of what happened to Carlos, and I see no purpose in digging for the truth. I imagine that he was caught up in a situation not entirely of his own making, and he was too embarrassed to let me know about it. I am certain that Carlos was not guilty of the charges against him in 1988, and I know it was right to seek justice for him. Of course, I am a little saddened at the ending of the story, but perhaps it is not over yet.

For me, these years have seen many blessings and some sadness. Susan Timken, my dear friend and business partner, died of cancer in November 1997, three years after we closed the bookstore. My mother died in March 1998, twenty-four hours after falling and breaking her hip in two places. It was exactly the way she wanted to go: living independently in her own home until the day she died, her mind sharp as a tack. Her spirit will always be with me.

On the blessings side, I have been with a wonderful man for seventeen years (my previous record was eighteen months). I met Jack through Mike Keating, who was his college roommate at Williams College. When Jack moved to Boston in 1992, two years after Carlos was freed, Mike told him to go into the bookstore and introduce himself. Mike swears he had no matchmaking motive, but that seems hard to believe. Jack is the love of my life, and I never would have met him if I hadn't intervened to help Carlos and gotten to know Mike. And I might not have been able to let him into my heart.

My life took a dramatic turn because of Carlos. The experience opened my eyes and my heart, and it set me free from myself, allowing me to accept true love when it came into my life. I often think how much poorer my life would have been if I had chosen another day for my postponed jury duty. I cannot imagine it. Whatever it was that led me into that courtroom, fate or mere chance, I am grateful.

ACKNOWLEDGEMENTS

Many people have helped me with *Lone Holdout*, both in living the story and in writing about it. I will always be grateful to Ed DeMore, Mike Keating, and Gary Crossen — the Three White Knights — and to my family and friends, who gave me such loyal support. My thanks go once more to all those who donated money to help win freedom for a man they did not know.

The book took twenty years and many drafts to write, beginning shortly after the events in the story. *Lone Holdout*, the final version, benefitted from the perspective of time and the help of others. Book consultant Pamela Painter gave me superb guidance in revising the manuscript; her expertise and encouragement were invaluable. I am grateful to Alexandra Marshall for recommending Pamela to me. The sharp eyes and sound advice of my friends and talented editors Jane Copass and Emily Shenk improved the manuscript immeasurably. Graphic designer Joanne Legge was an ideal partner, bringing skill, creativity, and patience to the making of the book.

My sister, Susan Mount, has been a loving and wise presence through it all. My life partner, Jack Kroh, patiently read many drafts and was always there to hold my hand.

CPSIA information can be obtained at www.ICGtesting.com
Printed in the USA
BVOW08s1857131113

336205BV00001B/62/P

9 780984 373307